C(

of

Heaven

for Beginners

Courts of Heaven

for Beginners

Ronald Montijn

Published by Seraph Creative

Courts of heaven for beginners

A practical guide for presenting your case in the courts of heaven

Author: Ronald Montijn

Advise: Arjan Hulsbergen, Meindert Van

Editor: Jim Bryson

Cover design: Feline Graphics

www.felinegraphics.com

ISBN 978-0-6485847-0-4

2nd Print English edition, 2019

Endorsements

It is with great pleasure that I endorse Ronald's primer on the courts of heaven. When I was first exposed to this approach to intercession, grave doubts arose in my mind about the legitimacy. I was wrestling with a financial blockage and a mutual friend introduced me to Beverley Watkins. I agreed to a prayer session on Skype two years ago. It was that experience in God's presence that changed my heart and then my mind. Since then Beverley and I have prayed with dozens of people over Skype and in person – all with powerful results.

Then, in the fall of 2017, we undertook coming to the Netherlands and opening the book of this great nation. What we found was an exciting destiny for this "gateway to Europe" to play her role in the next reformation. It was during that trip that Ronald drove down to Eindhoven and met with us. Like Beverley, he carries over a decade of experience in intercession and is very well-versed in the courts. It was like meeting someone we already knew. As we talked, I took a prophetic peek into Ron's book and destiny. Here's what I found…

This reformation will involve every mountain and it will bless nations. It will go far beyond our rather passive traditions of prayer and revival. I think of it as "Intention Reformation." Strategic men and women from business, politics, the arts, media, and education (every sector of our culture) will embrace their mandate to disciple nations. Jesus is the King of kings and these people will contend for their land and their personal kingdom assignments.

Courts of Heaven for Beginners will be a strategic tool for each of us to inherit our book… and Ronald will be a voice of practical guidance to show us how. Kings in the marketplace are being equipped with their priestly tools to open the heavens and bless the nations. So, I am blessing this book and this brother to do all that is in your heart, for the sake of the kingdom and for people like me.

John Garfield
www.releasingkings.com Kennewick, Washington USA, October 2017

The *Courts of Heaven for Beginners* is an invaluable tool in the hands of every believer who wants to advance in their destiny in God. Ronald has explained the foundational concepts and protocols of the court with great accuracy and excellence. His book is a much-needed exposition that will help God's people to understand both the doctrine and the spiritual "how-to" of this dimension of prayer.

In the Body of Christ, there are many people teaching on the courts of heaven, but few have the depth of insight and practical experience that is elucidated in this book. I highly recommend *Courts of Heaven for Beginners* to all who would seek to deal with the legal issues holding them back from walking in the fullness of destiny that Jesus won for them at the cross!

Beverley Watkins
Global Reformers-International Director for Africa
Johannesburg SA, October 2017

Ronald is an energetic and vibrant person. This has been well reflected in his unique ability to take a principle, explain and break it down into layman's language, giving the reader insight and knowledge on how YHVH functions.

His book will challenge and inspire readers of all ages in their growth and walk with the Father. I would recommend his book if you want this inspiration and out-working in your life.

Ian Clayton
Son of Thunder
www.sonofthunder.org

Content

Preface

One day I was driving through the beautiful center of Leuven, a Flemish[1] student town in Belgium. I guided the car absent-mindedly, preoccupied in conversation with the work acquaintance who was riding with me. I later discovered I had driven through a red light, as a substantial fine was delivered to my Dutch doormat a few weeks later.

I was momentarily tempted to neglect this judicial correction by the Flemish judicial authority, but my conscience quickly spoke against it. I had driven through a red light and was clearly at fault. This was a serious offence in Flanders. As I read the sobering subpoena, I became aware I now needed to give my account of the error in a court of law.

Instinctively, I understood it would be best to comply with these demands. I decided to appear in the Leuven court and was scheduled for a Friday morning at half past eight. This was quite exciting for me; I had never been in a courtroom before.

I was up before the sun to begin my trek down the Veluwe[2], reporting promptly to a stately and stale-smelling courtroom in Leuven. I shifted nervously as I took a seat on the row of other Flemish traffic offenders. No doubt they wondered what this stingy Dutchman was doing here. I waited patiently until it was my turn to appear before cantonal judge in Leuven.

As I sat, I reflected on what I had learned from Ronald's teaching about the courts of heaven. I had prepared myself, knowing that earthly courts operate under the jurisdiction of the heavenly courts and not apart from them. I knew that an earthly court had to be a reflection of the heavenly one. The judgments and verdicts on earth were called to be in line with the judgment and verdict rendered in heaven.

---

[1] Flanders is the northern part of Belgium. The main language is Dutch. Leuven is a city in Flanders. The people are called Flemish and they are convinced that the Dutch are stingy.

[2] The Veluwe is a beautiful rural part of the Netherlands and approximately a 3-hour drive from Leuven.

I am a beginner, I thought by myself, *but I'm going to practice this teaching and see what happens.* I had been praying and preparing my case at home, just as Ronald details in this book. I went in my spirit to the heavenly courtroom. I confessed my sins there and asked for a judgment. To be honest, I found it difficult to imagine a courtroom with a judge, prosecutor and defense lawyer. I had never been in a real courtroom. I did all this in steps of faith. As I prayed, I felt an impression that my arrival in Belgium, as well as the reason for my work in Leuven, would play a part in the judicial weighing of this case.

Suddenly, the courtroom door before me swung open. I, along with the other offenders, was sharply commanded by an officer with a Flemish accent to be silent. We were not to speak unless someone asked a question, or we would be removed from court. We were then ushered into a large, dusty hall. The judge's domineering bench stood in the middle, before whom cowered a handful of humble wooden benches for those on trial. The shabby room was lit just well enough to conclude that the entire thing could use a fresh coat of paint.

We all slid compliantly into our wooden seats. Abruptly, the judge prosecutor and scribe entered the courtroom. Everybody was summoned to rise as the court was called into session. The suspects individually pled their cases, represented by young lawyers. One by one, they received their verdicts.

All of a sudden, I was ordered to step forward. "So, mister Leeuwestein, where are you coming from?" the judge asked in Flemish. I answered through a thin, tight voice that I had come from Holland.

His eyebrows furrowed. he looked pointedly at the clock, did some quick math and turned his gaze back on me. "Hmm," he said. "It's not often that someone comes all the way from Holland to Leuven to pay a fine. What were you doing here the day you drove through the red light?"

The hall was deadly quiet, and the prosecutor and scribe stared at me. "I had an appointment for my work here, Your Honor," all the while trying to remember if a Flemish judge is even called "Your Honor." *Oh well, the extra respect can't hurt.*

"And just what kind of job do you have, mister Leeuwestein?" he pressed.

"I work for a foundation that supports persecuted Christians in countries like North Korea or Iran. We seek prayer and financial support from the churches in Leuven," I answered, my tone clear and respectful.

The judge's countenance changed immediately. Genuine interest spread across his face, so lightened that it seemed as though the Holy Spirit was resting upon him. The atmosphere in the courtroom entirely changed as he asked more questions about the persecution of Christians. Finally, he sat back in his chair.

"So, you were actually in Leuven to do something good when you drove through the red light. And this morning you drove three hours to answer to me as your judge. Is this summary correct?" he asked.

"That is correct, Your Honor," I confirmed quietly.

"Well, this is not something we see often here, mister Leeuwestein. And frankly, I find this highly remarkable."

The judge quietly consulted with the prosecutor for a few moments, then turned to me with obvious appreciation. "I declare you guilty for committing this offence but acquit you of any fine," he announced loudly. With a loud bang, his gavel struck the bench. "Next case."

Before I knew it, I was standing outside the courtroom, still not fully comprehending what just happened. I was guilty as charged but acquitted from the consequences. The judge had done exactly as I had prayed he would. I was astonished. I not only experienced my first encounter with the reality of the court system, but also experienced God's presence as Judge.

Through this, the Lord taught me that though I cannot do whatever I want without facing consequences, the verdicts in the courts of heaven are real. The experience opened my eyes for the tangible reality of God's authority.

I am only beginning to learn these truths about the courts of heaven. I want to encourage you not only to gain knowledge about it, but also to bring it into practice, especially when it concerns injustices done to you and to your family.

The Heavenly Judge wants to render a verdict in your favor. He is frustrated when the only testimony heard in court is that of the accuser.

Jesus Christ is our Advocate and assists us in our court cases. It is time to experience the Heavenly Judge as He executes judgment on your behalf.

This book will be a great help to you. Read it attentively and regularly and study the principles in the Word of God. And then, most importantly, apply them. There will be many wonderful breakthroughs that exceed my example. My prayer is that Ronald's book will be a great blessing, not only for you, but also for the ones that God has entrusted to you.

Sven Leeuwestein
Director IMPACT Navigators, The Netherlands
Elburg, October 2017

Introduction

The Courts of Heaven: Is This Something New?

About ten years ago, Ian Clayton began to teach about the existence and operation of the courts of heaven.[3] The Holy Spirit used him as a forerunner to prepare the way for the Body of Christ. The truths about these courts, which have been hidden for centuries, are now made available to the general public. It seems as if the heavenly books, which were sealed for a long time, have now been opened.[4]

More recently, other books have been written about the courts of heaven. Conferences are being held all over the world, in which Christians are trained to pray in the courts of heaven. Ministers are increasingly making teachings about the courts of heaven available to the larger Christian public. One such minister is Robert Henderson.

In 2015, Robert Henderson was invited to speak about this subject at a conference in the Netherlands. The Dutch translation of his book was presented at this conference.[5] In this book, Robert lays a foundation for the spiritual activities in the spiritual dimension. He explains the voices which plead on our behalf in the courts of heaven.

In all this we see a movement of God on the earth. In addition to the revelation that God is our Father, we also get to know Him as the Righteous Judge of the earth, a Judge that is longing to grant us justice.

---

[3] Ian is a prophetic pioneering teacher from New Zealand, who has been teaching about the heavenly dimensions for over 24 years; see www.sonofthunder.org.
[4] Daniel 12:9-10
[5] Procederen in de hemelse rechtbanken, Published by Mandate Publishing, 2015

A Challenge for The Reader

As the title indicates, this is a book for beginners. Beginners long to discover more about the existence of the courts of heaven and want to experience God vindicating them. These are the ones who truly want to be active in the courts of heaven, in order to see the kingdom of heaven being established on the earth. They are willing to stretch themselves to become mature sons in Christ and to grow in taking up responsibilities.

This book will be a challenge for you. It is not possible to stay passive when you read this book; you are being challenged to become active. I am asking a lot of you, and not simply to complete the assignments. I am also asking you to stay on board until you have finished the book. Your convictions may be challenged, especially if you have a different opinion about some of the insights mentioned in this book.

The goal of this book is to give you a practical guide in order to help you to present your own case to the Heavenly Judge in the courts of heaven. Therefore, it is important to read carefully and make yourself entirely familiar with the information presented here.

This book has two parts. In the first half, the biblical foundation for the existence and operation of the courts of heaven is laid. In the second half, you will prepare your own plea in the courts of heaven and present your case to the Heavenly Judge.

Now is the time to become active. This is your life, and you are the only person who can change it. The Father has invited you to enter the courts of heaven with Him.[6] There, He vindicates us all, so that we experience victory in our lives, and deals with every adversary that is hindering us to walk in our destiny.

Answers to Probing Questions

The courts of heaven are just as real as those on the earth. The judgments are binding, and the verdicts are real. But I can imagine that you still have tons of questions about this subject. Do these courts really

---

[6]   Isaiah 43:26

exist, or is it just my imagination? How do I enter these courts? What is the right protocol to follow? How does this all work? What is in it for me? Isn't the sacrifice of Jesus sufficient enough? This book works to answer these and many other questions.

There is also a workbook available. It will be a useful tool to complete the assignments laid out in this book. Some of these assignments are done just once, like writing the content of your own destiny scroll. But the other assignments are unique to each time you enter the courts of heaven to plead your case. The workbook assists you in preparation for every time you go to court.

An Open Hand

In the last few years, I have obtained more insight and respect for the manner in which the Jewish people honor the words of the Most High. They have intensely studied His words for thousands of years. Let us learn from them in this, putting aside our prejudices. I hope that we as western Christians begin to understand the depths that are hidden inside the Word of God.

The rabbis teach us that there are seventy different interpretations for every passage of Scripture. All these contain truth and can exist next to each other.[7] This expresses the richness and depths of our God and of His Word. Most of the time, the Jewish people welcome someone with a different opinion. They embrace new perspectives because each new facet enables them to learn something new of God in a new truth that they have never seen before.

Of course, you are entitled to have different opinions about parts of this book or have different experiences. But please do not become offended by what you read. Instead, receive the message of this book with an open heart and an open hand.

I testify in this book about the things I have seen about the greatness of our God, the Creator of heaven and earth, the King of the universe, Adonai Eloheinu, who sent His Son, Yeshua HaMashiach to the world to

---

[7]   The term for this concept of multiple interpretation is Shiv'im panim laTorah (Each verse of Torah has seventy different faces or facets.).

Of course, you are entitled to have different opinions about parts of this book or have different experiences. But please do not become offended by what you read. Instead, receive the message of this book with an open heart and an open hand.

I testify in this book about the things I have seen about the greatness of our God, the Creator of heaven and earth, the King of the universe, Adonai Eloheinu, who sent His Son, Yeshua HaMashiach to the world to redeem and to deliver us, Who gave His Spirit Ruach Ha-Kodesh to live inside of us, by which we are being let into the fullness He has prepared for us.

As you read this book, it is my desire that your walk of faith will be enriched and your relationship with the Father, the Son and the Holy Spirit deepened. That there will come an end to the injustice that exists in your life. That you are able to present your case to the Heavenly Judge and that He will vindicate you. That you will have victory over every enemy in your life. That you will experience freedom and will realize the destiny God has given you. That you will discover new aspects of His government. That you will know what it is to stand in creation as a son of God. That you will experience the fullness of the mercy and freedom that was promised to us.

Ronald Montijn
Duivendrecht, October 22, 2017

Part 1

Biblical Foundation

1

There Is Nothing New Under the Sun

There is nothing new under sun, the Preacher once said. That which has been is what will be. That which is done is what will be done.[9] These words deeply express the mind of Jewish culture. In sharp contrast to the Greek manner of thinking, the Jews view the ages in a circular manner.

Greek thinking is linear: $1 + 2 + 3 = 6$. But for the Jews, the end must equal the beginning: $1 + 2 + 3 = 6 = 3 + 2 + 1$. Creation itself is in equilibrium; there is order and balance to it. We see this manner of thinking when Jesus said to His disciples: *The coming of the Son of Man at the end of the world will be like the days of Noah.* In the last days, we will see the same things happening as in the days of Noah. As one example, think of our current discussions about gender. The same thing happened back then and was one of the reasons the earth was flooded.

> *But as the days of Noah were, so also will the coming of the Son of Man be. For as in the days before the flood, they were eating and drinking, marrying and giving in marriage, until the day that Noah entered the ark, and did not know until the flood came and took them all away, so also will the coming of the Son of Man be.*
> *Matthew 24:37-39*

What does this mean for us as Christians? For starters, it helps us to understand that the circumstances in this world are of no surprise for God. We might experience something as new or even revolutionary, but all things are absolutely no secret to Him. Sometimes it is God's glory to conceal a matter, but it is the glory of kings to search out a matter.[10] He invites us to learn from Him and to be led by Him. It is His desire to reveal these secrets to us.

The speed by which new revelations are brought into the church has only seemed to increase in recent years. Historically, new concepts took

---

9   Ecclesiastics 1:9
10 Proverbs 25:2

years to learn and spread. But nowadays, the latest revelation hasn't even been fully shared when the next is already knocking on the door. Some Christians run from one conference to another and seem to have nothing else to do than to hunt down the latest new thing. They look a lot like the Athenians in the days of Paul.[11] Other Christians feel troubled by these developments. Their frame of reference is insufficient to judge what to accept and what to reject. This makes them uncertain or fearful, and fear is a bad counselor.

Fear of Deception

When it comes to the acceptance of new ideas, products, or teaching, we often just wait and see what happens. We decide to let someone else be first to prove that it works or that it is safe. There's nothing wrong with that because we are all different. Some of us are forerunners, while others wait to see which way the wind blows. But be aware that we all have a deeply rooted fear of deception in our hearts. When we act out of this fear, we are at risk of missing the good things that the Father wants to give us.

Where does this fear originate? It is one of the consequences of the fall in the garden. Mankind lost their innocence when Adam ate from the forbidden tree. The disappointment Adam and Eve experienced in being driven out of the garden caused a great fear of deception. They made, so to speak, an inner vow: "Never again will we be deceived by this enemy!" This conviction has attached itself to their inner being and passed through the bloodline to every human being ever since. The result? Many of us watch the new developments in the kingdom of God from afar. We are afraid to make the same mistake Adam and Eve made.

This book probably contains new insights for you. I am asking you to engage them with an open heart. By definition, new revelations and insights have no precedent. After all, they are new. Conversely, your convictions and insights about what is true are based on the revelations and impressions from the past. To discover something new, you not only need to have an open mind, but also have the intention to weigh the content and test it.

---

[11] Acts 17:21

Furthermore, don't become distracted by the way the message is offered to you. I recently shared an article on Facebook about a political situation in America. I was surprised that the resulting discussion did not refer to the content of the article, but instead vilified the news site that published it. Commenters said the reporting was poor and unbalanced.

This kind of reasoning can happen to all of us. We don't change our prejudices and mindsets easily, and our opinions are often based more upon our frame of reference than an accurate conclusion of the facts.

When we study the life of Jesus, we see many times that His message offended the people.[12] Could it be that God wants to test our hearts in order to see if we really want to go for the hidden treasure? This is what Paul meant when he said that the cross was a stumbling block to the Jews.[13] Are we able to see the hidden treasures inside the message?

What Is Our Frame of Reference?

When we want to judge new insights, we need to have a sound frame of reference. What do I mean by that? Our knowing, in understanding and insight, is limited. After all, we are not God. How then can we be sure that these new developments are safe? How do we discern if something is from God or is just deception?

Of course, our first touchstone is the Bible. In it, we find the guidelines for a holy life just as they were given to us by the Almighty One. The Bible keeps us on track in matters concerning our behavior and our relationship with God.

But how do we deal with new technological developments, or with insights we can't discern with our natural senses? Does the Bible talk about this also? The question of "Where is this in the Bible?" is sincere, but this kind of questioning can also limit us. Nobody is all-knowing except God. God wraps Himself in secrets, but it is up to us to discover these secrets.[14] We all have experienced new discoveries in Scripture, although we have studied it for years. When this happens, it is as though a veil has been

---

[12] Matthew 13:57; Mark 14:27; John 6:60-66
[13] 1 Corinthians 1:23
[14] Proverbs 25:2

removed, and now we see the new revelation. Instantly, we feel as though everybody needs to hear it.

When Jesus walked on the earth, the Scribes and Pharisees often attacked Him. Based on their knowledge and understanding, they had concluded that Jesus could never be the promised Messiah. It was *their* conviction that many of the things He did and said were against the commandants God had given them. Jesus became a threat to them because He didn't comply with their interpretation of the Tenach. He simply didn't meet their expectation of the Messiah. Their frame of reference was too narrow.

> They answered and said to Him, "Are you also from Galilee? Search and look, for no prophet has arisen out of Galilee."
>
> *John 7:52*

It is easy to be wise after the event. We read the stories in the Bible through the eyes of someone who knows the outcome. There is really no escape from this. Church history shows us that when it comes to new insights, forerunners and opponents compete with each other in every generation. There are many examples in the last century concerning revelations that were controversial at first but are now more widely accepted.

God wraps Himself in secrets,
but it is up to us to discover these secrets.

For example: speaking in tongues, healing ministry, women in church leadership positions, spiritual warfare, and the role of apostles and prophets in the church. Often, the establishment struggles to let go of old convictions and to embrace the new. Most of the time, their resistance is rooted in the price these men and women of God had to pay for their revelation. They are the carriers of the old revelation and have a deep sense of responsibility for it. Letting go of that can be very difficult.

The First Council in Jerusalem

The first council of the Apostles in Jerusalem, as described in Acts 15, is one of our greatest examples of how to deal with new insights. Paul and Barnabas were sent out by the council of the Apostles to proclaim the gospel to the heathen. While traveling through Asia, they came to the conclusion that circumcision was no longer necessary for new believers. In fact, Paul stated that for every person who became circumcised, Christ would be no profit to them at all.

> *Indeed I, Paul, say to you that if you become circumcised, Christ will profit you nothing. And I testify again to every man who becomes circumcised that he is a debtor to keep the whole law.*
>
> *Galatians 5:2-3*

A large group of Pharisees had joined the followers of Jesus in Jerusalem, but when Paul returned with this teaching, they were furious. Paul wasn't just any rabbi. The Pharisees regarded him with high esteem; after all, he sat at the feet of Gamaliel, a qualification of deep influence in their circles.[15] You didn't just apply to become a disciple of Gamaliel. You had to be asked, and you had to be the best of the best. Some even venture that Paul was destined to become the new leader of the Pharisees one day. Do you now understand why they became so angry when he presented this controversial teaching?

> *And when they had come to Jerusalem, they were received by the church and the apostles and the elders; and they reported all things that God had done with them. But some of the sect of the Pharisees who believed rose up, saying, "It is necessary to circumcise them, and to command them to keep the law of Moses."*
>
> *Acts 15:4-5*

Their point of view is very understandable. After all, the law of Moses clearly stated that new converts had to be circumcised.[16] It was written in their Tenach. However, the Holy Spirit had shown Paul that circumcision would not benefit the new believers. The act of circumcision would actually be a hindrance, not freedom, to them.

And this is exactly the point. In Hebrew, *Torah* means "instructions," and not "law" as we commonly think. In the Torah—the first five books of the Old Testament that were given to Moses—we find the guidelines

---

[15] Gamaliel was a very influential rabbi and presided in the Sanhedrin. He was the grandson of the famous rabbi Hillel, who had a special authority to explain the Torah and was regarded with the highest esteem. Gamaliel' disciples were, therefore, also very influential among the Pharisees.

[16] Exodus 12:48

for a healthy, secure, and above all, sanctified life. The Torah is much more than an enumeration of do's and don'ts.

The Holy Spirit can give a new revelation that supersedes written instruction and shines a different light upon Scripture. Many Christians find this difficult, often because their faith and their choices in life are based upon *their* interpretation of the letter of the law and not on a living relationship with the Creator. This, combined with the fear of deception, is the breeding ground for the most destructive spirit mankind has ever known: the religious spirit. After all, it is this spirit that incited the Pharisees to kill Jesus.

There is a risk involved when we live in freedom and out of grace.[17] We will make mistakes and some of them could have great consequences. Having said that, we can't avoid making choices. When we do not act because we fear we might be deceived, we might later realize that we have resisted the Spirit of the Living God. That is why Gamaliel gave this counsel to the rulers of the Sanhedrin.

> *"And now I say to you, keep away from these men and let them alone; for if this plan or this work is of men, it will come to nothing; but if it is of God, you cannot overthrow it—lest you even be found to fight against God."*
>
> Acts 5:38-39

How Do We Examine New Insights?

How then ought we to deal with these new insights and revelations? I mentioned before that the Bible is the foundation of our lives and our convictions. However, the Spirit of the living God can give us insights that make new depths of the Word of God come alive. Paul indicated that he walked closely with the Holy Spirit; they agreed together.[18] This is a unity that you can experience, and it is a touchstone.

How should we judge new insights or revelations to see if they are inspired by the Holy Spirit or not? A test that is based on our interpretation of the Word might appear adequate, but history shows that church splits are mainly caused by holding on to one's own explanation of Scripture.

---

[17] See The Grace Awakening from Charles R. Swindoll, 1990.
[18] Acts 15:28

It is important to be brutally honest, especially when we look at ourselves. To what extent have we dealt with the fear of deception that is inside our DNA?[19] How much influence does your culture have on your decision-making process? Do your spiritual leaders factor into your thinking? Sometimes we know the right thing to do, but our insecurity and fear, or the influences of our culture or community, influence us to choose otherwise.

In many aspects, the teachings of Jesus were revolutionary. Everyone had their opinion, resulting in fierce discussions. When Jesus was questioned about the source of His teaching, His answer was astonishing.

> *Jesus answered them and said, "My doctrine is not Mine, but His who sent Me. If anyone wills to do His will, he shall know concerning the doctrine, whether it is from God or whether I speak on My own authority."*
>
> *John 7:16-17*

The only way to discover if Jesus is telling the truth is to do as He says. Only then will we discover whether or not His doctrine is from God. Therefore, it is impossible to discover the truth by reasoning only. Reason, by definition, is an activity of our soul. Only the human spirit can get to the bottom of the mysteries of God.[20] You have to find out for yourself before you make a decision. It would be heartbreaking to reject a revelation that God has specifically brought into your path.

The manner in which you investigate is also very important. Don't try to prove something wrong or simply unbiblical. Openly investigate it, as the Bereans did. Using Scripture, they tried to prove that the teaching of Paul was *true*. If you can't, try harder.

> *These were more fair-minded than those in Thessalonica, in that they received the word with all readiness, and searched the Scriptures daily to find out whether these things were so.*
>
> *Acts 17:11*

---

[19] DNA is the carrier of our hereditary information. Our appearance, our character, and our preferences are mainly determined by our DNA. We carry, in our DNA, the consequences for the choices our ancestors made.

[20] 1 Corinthians 2:13-16

Essential Characteristics

We will not easily be deceived when we stay close to the Father, the Son, and the Holy Spirit. You can use the following characteristics to discover if a new revelation is from God.

When we walk with the Father, we experience His judgment, holiness, and righteousness.

But the Lord of Hosts shall be exalted in judgment, and God who is holy shall be hallowed in righteousness.

Isaiah 5:16

Walk with Jesus and try to discover if His characteristics are there. Does it bring the truth? Does it lead you on the living way to God?

Jesus said to him, "I am the way, the truth, and the life. No one comes to the Father except through Me."

John 14:6

The characteristics of the Holy Spirit are righteousness, peace, and joy. When these are strengthened by the revelation, you are on the right track.

For the kingdom of God is not eating and drinking, but righteousness and peace and joy in the Holy Spirit.

Romans 14:17

Our adversary has only one goal: to destroy our relationship with God. He uses ungodly beliefs that are fed by our fears, the lies in our mind, and influences from our culture.

Ask: Does this revelation lead me to the heart of the Father?

Ask: Is the truth being made public, and will I be made free when I act on it?

Ask: Does the revelation change my life for the better?

Ask: Does the revelation strengthen my relationship with the Holy Spirit?

You may have noticed that righteousness is a characteristic both of the Father and the Holy Spirit. While this is true, there is a difference. The righteousness from the Father is seen from the position of the Judge, as the one who is the upholder of justice. The Holy Spirit sees righteousness from our position, as one who has transgressed the law. He is pleading on our behalf to the Father and gives Him the arguments to give us righteousness.

When you learn to apply these nine characteristics, you will see that the risk of getting lost will disappear before your eyes. Just keep asking yourself the questions that are based upon these divine characteristics. Does this revelation bring the righteousness of God into your life? Will the truth of Christ be revealed? Do you experience the peace and joy of the Holy Spirit?

Conclusion

Contemplate this revelation about the courts of heaven with an open mind, even if you have never heard of it before. Investigate and search the Scriptures in order to prove that this revelation is true. That is the right attitude. The ability to arrive at your own conclusion is a characteristic of maturity. When new revelations, new ways of thinking, or changes in doctrine are bombarding the church, you can't simply look to your leaders to give you an answer.

As a mature son or daughter of God, you should be able to make decisions concerning your own life. This is especially true when dealing with matters that are not observed by our natural senses. You need to have a stable frame of reference. Of course, you can consult your friends and leaders about your conclusions, but every person is responsible for their own walk with the Lord.

In light of this, learn to use the touchstones that are mentioned in this chapter. In a sound revelation, the characteristics should not only be present but also in harmony with each other. Just like tuning a guitar before you start playing, is it important to tune these touchstones. Remember that sometimes you will only discover afterward if the decision you made was correct. That's called walking in faith.

Don't be passive. Reach out for a living relationship with God the Father, the Son, and the Holy Spirit. It is out of this relationship that you will receive the courage to go forward.

You cannot assume that new insights are wrong just because they are new. Someone may have an important key for your life. Learn to investigate it. Let us move forward in love, accepting and respecting each other.

In the next chapter, I will discuss the relation we have with God as Judge.

2

We Need God to Be Our Judge

Before we continue to study the courts of heaven, it is important to discuss the relationship we have with God. In the Bible, we see that God is called our Father, Friend, and Judge. Robert Henderson explains this in his first book[21], about the courts of heaven. The roles of father and judge reflect someone who is in a position of authority over us, a concept that can be difficult to embrace for those who have had a negative experience with authority in life. But we all have someone who is positioned over us, whether that be in our family, in school, or in our work, and sometimes we resist them because of the negative experiences we have had with people in authority.

In the last few years, many Father's Heart conferences and schools have been held in the Netherlands. Many people have experienced a restoration in their view about God as their Father. It is such a blessing for the body of Christ that the image of God as a Father is being restored.

Some find it difficult to experience God as their friend, as someone with whom they can share life's joy and sorrows. They can embrace the idea of Jesus as their friend but viewing God as their friend brings Him too close for comfort. They can find healing when they have a personal experience of the Father's love.

But now we look to God as Judge. When we are summoned to appear before a judge, some of us become not only uncomfortable but also very afraid. Part of this has to do with our Calvinistic background, where our God is portrayed as a stern and angry person. This God is distant and is constantly looking for the mistakes we make in our lives; above all else, This is a God that we need to fear, one who is always ready to pour out His wrath upon us at the moment we do something wrong. This line of thinking is expressed in the Dutch proverb: "God punishes immediately."

---

[21] Operating in the Courts of Heaven by Robert Henderson

This pattern of belief convinces us that God constantly reminds us of our shortcomings and failures. This God isn't merciful at all.

But this picture of an angry, severely-punishing ruler doesn't resemble the Creator at all. And yet this perspective is often deeply embedded in our emotions, even in our DNA. The moment we hear the word "judgment" we think about punishment and try to ease our guilty consciences by developing reasonable excuses.

One day I was walking with a colleague during a break at work. We talked about many things, including our jobs and our faith. During the conversation, I shared with him that I had asked God to judge me. I did this because I wanted to know what He thought about my life. My friend was shocked, sincerely upset that I dared to ask something like this of God. My friend declared he would never make such a request to God.

Many would react the same way my friend did. As soon as they hear the word "judging" they become so afraid that they distance themselves from God. They hide from Him just like Adam and Eve did.

And they heard the sound of the Lord God walking in the garden in the cool of the day, and Adam and his wife hid themselves from the presence of the Lord God among the trees of the garden. Then the Lord God called to Adam and said to him, "Where are you?" So he said, "I heard Your voice in the garden, and I was afraid because I was naked; and I hid myself."

Genesis 3:8-10

We often behave in the same manner, a reflex that has been passed through our bloodline having entered our DNA through Adam. Our DNA is the carrier of all hereditary information. This means that virtues *and* vices are passed on from parents to children. That is why our children often show the same behavior as other relatives, even if they have never seen or met them.

There is a way out of this situation, however: repentance and the blood of the Lamb. Honestly confess to God that you become afraid when you face Him as Judge. Be open about the fear you experience as soon as you have the impression that you are being judged. Repent from the fear of rejection and the fear of being punished.

God Is Our Judge

If we give it quiet thought, we see that it is strange that we would experience such a deeply-rooted fear of someone we desperately need. This is one of the tactics of our adversary, satan. He has succeeded in creating a resistance deep in our emotions toward the God who alone is capable of redeeming us. In this, we can learn so much from David. David was not afraid of God; instead, David saw Him as a place of refuge.

The Lord is my rock and my fortress and my deliverer; my God, my strength, in whom I will trust; my shield and the horn of my salvation, my stronghold. I will call upon the Lord, who is worthy to be praised; so shall I be saved from my enemies.

Psalm 18:2-3

If anyone understood what it meant to be persecuted in their innocence, it would be David. As a boy, he was rejected by his family. In the court of Saul, he was initially welcomed with cheers but in the end, Saul was trying to kill him. Though he was innocent, he was chased away. All of his life his enemies were constantly trying to kill him.

> That is why David calls upon God as Judge,
> to vindicate him.

When David is in trouble, he calls upon the name of the Lord, and not just to be comforted or to be delivered from his problems. No, above any other function, David turns to God as Judge; only in that capacity is God able to help him. As a Father, God can comfort him, and as a Friend, He can help him in the battles of his life, but only as Judge can He vindicate him against his enemies.

David knew that the kingdom of God was founded upon a judicial system. God's laws and regulations authorize everything that happens in the kingdom. If you act well, you will receive a reward, and if you transgress, you will receive a reprimand. That is why David calls upon God as Judge — to vindicate him, or if necessary, to convict, purge, and purify him.

Save me, O God, by Your name, and vindicate me by Your strength. Hear my prayer, O God; give ear to the words of my mouth.

Psalm 54:1-2

When injustice has been done to us, we need a righteous Judge that will avenge us. Unfortunately, we are often stuck in the conviction that we too are somehow guilty.

If our conscience accuses or condemns us, we do not dare to approach God as Judge. We believe these lies of the enemy and we are stuck in our misery. But God invites us to go to court together. There, we will be justified. You must no longer allow the fear of punishment, deception, and condemnation have power over you.

> *I, yes I, am the one who blots out your offenses for my own sake; I will not remember your sins. Remind me when we're in court together— tell your side, make the case that you are right.*
>
> *Isaiah 43:25-26 (CJB)*

It is up to you to break the power that the enemy has over your emotions. Overcome this fear by going to God our Father, confessing that you find it difficult to see Him as your Judge. Ask Him to help you to overcome this fear. Then you will be able to approach God as Judge with a fearless heart, confident in He who justifies you.

The Lord, the Righteous Judge

The moment we understand that our redemption is the direct result of a court order, our fear of God as Judge disappears. All legal demands that are necessary for the reconciliation of man with God were fulfilled by the sacrifice of Jesus on the cross. The only legal ground upon which satan has to attack us is our own transgressions of the law and regulations of God. Didn't Jesus Himself say that when satan comes, he will find nothing? The ruler of this world couldn't find any legal ground in Jesus because He never sinned. He had never once transgressed the commandments of His Father, His King, and His Judge.

> *I will no longer talk much with you, for the ruler of this world is coming, and he has nothing in Me. But that the world may know that I love the Father,*
> *and as the Father gave Me commandment, so I do. Arise, let us go from here.*
>
> *John 14:30-31*

This is why satan couldn't do anything against Him. That is the reason the Bible specifies that His hour had not come. Only after Jesus took upon Himself all the sins of mankind did satan gain the legal right to torture and to kill Him. Until then, he couldn't do anything to Jesus.

Humanity came under the dominion of the evil one by the sin of one man. The redemption of humanity, on the other hand, was the result of the obedience of one man.[22] God obtained the legal right to acquit us from death by the sacrifice of Jesus Christ. We need to realize that our justification, our restoration, and our healing could only take place because there was a verdict from the righteous Judge. This verdict says: "Because the Son of God, Jesus Christ, took all sin upon Himself, you are justified from sin."

The only thing that is necessary to activate this verdict from the Judge is to acknowledge that Jesus Christ is the Lord of our lives. In that, we confess that we are crucified with Him, have died in Him, and have risen from the dead in Him.

> *Knowing this, that our old man was crucified with Him, that the body of sin might be done away, that so we should no longer be in bondage to sin; for He that hath died is justified from sin.*
>
> *Romans 6:6-7 (ASV)*

We are justified from sin. This means sin doesn't have any legal power over us. When we confess our sins, the evil one has no more power over us. He can't do anything to us anymore. It is very important that we understand that the legal status "justified from sin" is directly connected to the confession of the sins in our lives. As long as we hide our sins and are silent about them, satan has the legal right to attack us. That is why David said that his freedom came after his confession.

> *I acknowledged my sin to You, and my iniquity I have not hidden. I said, "I will confess my transgressions to the Lord," And You forgave the iniquity of my sin. Selah. For this cause everyone who is godly shall pray to You in a time when You may be found; surely in a flood of great waters they shall not come near Him.*
>
> *Psalm 32:5-7*

---

[22] Romans 5:12-19

When God forgives us our sins as Judge, He renders a verdict and justifies us from sin. After all, the adversary accuses us day and night.[23] Do we realize that when we confess our sins, this confession is recorded in a heavenly court?

The forgiveness of our sins is directly connected to our confession. As long as we are silent, our adversary has power over us. Doesn't Jesus say that when we are on our way to a court with our adversary, we must agree with him quickly?[24] This is the reason John calls us to confess our sins immediately because we have an advocate in heaven that pleas for us.

> *If we say that we have no sin, we deceive ourselves, and the truth is not in us. If we confess our sins, He is faithful and just to forgive us our sins and to cleanse us from all unrighteousness. If we say that we have not sinned, we make Him a liar, and His word is not in us. My little children, these things I write to you, so that you may not sin. And if anyone sins, we have an Advocate[25] with the Father, Jesus Christ the righteous. And He Himself is the propitiation for our sins, and not for ours only but also for the whole world.*
>
> *1 John 1:8-2:2*

Jesus knows the battle we are fighting against sin; He Himself has fought the same battle and He did not yield. Paul shows us something about this battle in Romans 7. He tells us about the struggle he is experiencing inside himself. He desperately wants to obey the law, but he fails every time. Then he cries out: "O wretched man that I am! Who will deliver me from this body of death?" His answer is: "Jesus Christ, our Lord." Our legal status has changed; we are acquitted by the Judge! We are no longer condemned.

> *There is therefore now no condemnation to those who are in Christ Jesus, who do not walk according to the flesh, but according to the Spirit.*
>
> *Romans 8:1*

---

23 Revelations 12:10
24 Matthew 5:25-26
25 In the Greek text we read here paraklétos, advocate, comforter, and helper. This is the same word by which the Holy Spirit is indicated in John 14:16,24.

God Doesn't Take Sides

What we must realize is that we appear in the courtroom of the Almighty God. It is His courtroom. He is the Judge; we are not. We approach Him because injustice has been done to us. The emotions can run high; we can be extremely angry or sad. But do not make the mistake of thinking that God as Judge will be persuaded to take our side or rule in our favor solely because He loves us. He doesn't take sides; when He is sitting on His throne, He is completely impartial.

> *For the Lord your God is God of gods and Lord of Lords, the great God, mighty and awesome, who shows no partiality nor takes a bribe. He administers justice for the fatherless and the widow, and loves the stranger, giving him food and clothing.*
>
> *Deuteronomy 10:17-18*

There is a great difference between the compassion that God has for us as a Father and the way He administers justice. His judgments are based on His legislation, the testimonies, and the evidence presented in court, and not because He likes us. It is His desire to administer justice and to deliver us from the accuser. That is His passion, which is His love in action. It is therefore critical to realize that God doesn't take our side, but that we must choose His side.

It is therefore so important to realize that God doesn't take our side, but that we must choose His side.

The Holy Spirit will plead for us when we appear for God. He will help us to better understand the position God has as Judge. We will have to agree with God and acknowledge that He judges with a righteous judgment. When we agree with God about the injustice that has been done to us, as well as our part in it, we will be acquitted from all charges.

The Role of Satan As Prosecutor

Did you know that Jesus didn't speak Greek to His disciples, but Aramaic? That was the contemporary language in those days. The writers of the Gospels were common people that had no special education. It is therefore plausible that the Gospels were first written in Aramaic and were later translated into Greek. By doing so, the good news became available for a larger public. This happens also today. The contemporary language on the internet is English and not Swahili.

Many of us are familiar with the Lord's Prayer; it is the prayer that Jesus taught His disciples when they asked Him how they should pray. In this prayer is a familiar sentence we know well, but when you read it in Aramaic it can have a completely different meaning. In the middle of the Lord's Prayer, Jesus says the following:

And do not lead us into temptation but deliver us from the evil one.
Matthew 6:13

The Greek word for temptation is *peirasmon*. This Greek is a translation of the original Jewish Aramaic word *mishaonah*. This word can mean "temptation", but it also means "trial, the legal kind in a court of law." Instead of asking God not to tempt us, we can read this very differently. We ask God not to bring us to trial, that is, not to take legal actions against us because of our sins.

In the second part of this verse, we ask God to deliver us from evil. When we continue the court of justice imagery, we can also read this as a request to the Judge. *Deliver me from the accuser.* In Jewish tradition, satan was not the ruler of all evil. He wasn't known as the prince of darkness, but as a fallen angel, obedient to God and subservient to Him.

His job was to act as a counsel for the prosecution as the accuser. He was the one who brought the charges into the court of heaven. When we appear before the judgment seat, our sins would be examined. Everything that we had done was tested according to the laws and regulations of the kingdom of heaven. It was the task of satan to present the evidence of our sins before the Judge. When we use this explanation[26] of this version we can read it like this:

And do not bring us to trial but deliver us from the accuser.
Matthew 6:13 (Aramaic translation)

In Hebrew as well as in Greek, satan means "accuser or adversary." He is the one that is accusing us day and night before our God.[27] He is

---

[26]   The original our Father in Jewish Aramaic:
        https://youtu.be/i8IJOgMVE1Q?t=4m50s
[27]   Revelations 12:10

constantly looking for evidence that testifies against us. He searches the heavenly dossiers, where everything that happened in our lives, the iniquities in our bloodline, and even our thoughts and considerations are recorded. These are the dossiers where all we have done on the earth is recorded and by which we will be judged.

> *And I saw the dead, small and great, standing before God, and books were opened. And another book was opened, which is the Book of Life. And the dead were judged according to their works, by the things which were written in the books.*
>
> *Revelations 20:12*

Keeping short accounts

This is why it is so important to understand that we have an Advocate who pleads for us. Jesus Christ intercedes for us in the courts of heaven. We only need to confess our sins in order to be acquitted from sin. When we confess our transgressions, the blood of the Lamb can operate for us. At that same moment, all our sins are blotted out of every heavenly dossier.[28] But any sin that we consciously conceal will be presented by the accuser as evidence before the Judge. This is the reason Jesus is urging us to quickly agree with our adversary. Because, when we stand before the Judge and there is still an open account, it will have consequences for us.

When we voluntarily go to court in order to confess our sins, the accuser can do nothing against us. The blood of Jesus protects us against his accusations. But when we keep silent and rationalize our sins, the adversary has enough evidence to get us convicted.[29]

Don't let it come to this! Keep short accounts. Agree quickly and make things right when someone has something against us. There should be no reason to be afraid to appear before the Judge when we live our lives like this. After all, we know that the blood of Christ speaks better things than that of Abel.[30] The blood of Abel spoke *from the earth* to God and called for revenge and vengeance.[31] The blood of the Lamb, though, speaks *from*

---

[28] Acts 3:19
[29] Matthew 5:25-26
[30] Hebrew 12:24
[31] Genesis 4:10

heaven. It pleads for us and asks for forgiveness because we didn't know what we were doing.

Conclusion

It is impossible to separate God as Judge and God as Father. After all, God is one. He reigns from His throne and He comes to us in the cool of the day to be our Father. Just as we can learn to experience God as our Father, we can also learn to experience Him as Judge. This Judge is not corrupt, and He is not against us. No, He is a righteous Judge who hates false testimony. What can be better than to have a Judge who favors us, one who is also our Father, our Friend, and who is willing to help us in our legal battle against our adversary? Even more, His Son is our wonderful Counselor, who pleads for us before the throne. Let us choose His side and acknowledge that He is absolutely impartial. Just as Isaiah did, let us reach out to the perfect Triune God who is for us.

> *For the Lord is our Judge, the Lord is our Lawgiver, the Lord is our King; He will save us.*
>
> *Isaiah 33:22*

In the next chapter, we will see examples from the Bible of when a court is in session.

3

The Courts of Heaven in the Bible

In recent years, many new insights about the structure of heaven have been made available to the church. We owe this especially to the teachings that Ian Clayton has been given in the last decade, elaborating on the way the government of the kingdom of heaven is structured.[32] An important element of any form of government is the manner in which the administration of justice is regulated.

The more I studied this subject, the more it seemed I had a completely new Bible in my hands. I found references about the heavenly court systems in many places and I suddenly had a clear understanding that God's government is an eternal government founded upon a legal system.

Of the increase of His government and peace there will be no end, upon the throne of David and over His kingdom, to order it and establish it with judgment and justice from that time forward, even forever. The zeal of the Lord of Hosts will perform this.

Isaiah 9:7

The foundations of His authority are righteousness and justice. When you realize that God as King is also the Judge of His creation, this truth will give you a completely new understanding.

When it comes to the interpretation of the Torah, Rashi is one of the greatest authoritative rabbis in this field.[33] He consequently translates the Hebrew word *Elohim* with "God the Judge." In his commentary[34] on the first three words of the Bible in Genesis 1:1, Rashi explains it as follows: "When (God the Judge) created for the first time." With this statement, the Torah proves that the foundation of creation is embedded in

---

[32] See the website of Ian Clayton for more information: www.sonofthunder.org.
[33] Rashi lived in France from 1040 until 1105. His commentary on the Torah has taken a central place in the Jewish education for the last 900 years.
[34] The Mystery of Creation according to Rashi, Moznaim Publication Corporation.

righteousness. Righteousness is the substance, the essence, and the foundation upon which this creation is seated.

As we mentioned earlier, creation is balanced to the Jewish mind. In order to balance the creating God who is a Judge, there must also be another God who creates. This balancing facet of the Lord appears in Genesis 2:4. The Hebrew name LORD is indicated by four Hebrew letters: *JHVH*. Rashi tells us that this name means: "God the merciful one."[35] The Torah expresses that the government of the Almighty God over His creation is rooted in righteousness *and* in mercy and grace. Can we now understand what John meant when he said that Jesus came in grace and truth?

For the law was given through Moses, but grace and truth came through Jesus Christ.

John 1:17

The Torah was given by God to Moses, but it was not fulfilled. Jesus Christ, who came in grace and truth, fulfilled the Torah. The Torah contains the essential characteristics of the legal systems in heaven. Therein lie the guidelines, instructions, and the consequences.[36] These are the foundation of His Government, but there is also grace and truth, and they come through Jesus Christ. This is why He is called our Advocate, our Lawyer.

Christ has come to restore the balance in creation. Besides the voice in heaven that is crying out for justice, there is now also a voice on the earth. This voice cries out for mercy and brings truth. Without mercy and truth, righteous government does not exist. It is crucial that we understand that the Almighty God can't transgress His own laws and regulations. The moment He doesn't keep His own laws, the foundation of His authority and government is broken. At that moment He would have to abdicate His throne.

Biblical concepts like "the ark of the Testimony," "the Counsel of the Lord," and "cancelled the charge of our legal indebtedness on the cross"[37] gain a whole different meaning when you see them in the context of a

---

[35] The Mystery of Creation according to Rashi, Moznaim Publication Corporation, 1982.
[36] Torah means instructions
[37] Exodus 26:33-34; Isaiah 19:17; Colossians 2:14

court session. Perhaps now we understand why God hates a false witness; that is why He wrote a whole law about it.[38]

It is crucial that we understand that the Almighty God
can't transgress His own laws and regulations.

We will now go on a journey through the Bible studying some examples of the court systems in heaven. This will give us better insight of how the government of the kingdom of heaven is established. Through this, we will learn to prepare our own court case, the ability for which is one of the main goals of this book. We must know that there is a God in heaven that will justify us when we ask Him to do so.[39]

The Vision of Daniel

We start our journey in the book of Daniel, chapter 7. Daniel describes a vision where he sees a court in session and books are opened.

> *I watched till thrones were put in place, and the Ancient of Days was seated; His garment was white as snow, and the hair of His head was like pure wool. His throne was a fiery flame, its wheels a burning fire; A fiery stream issued and came forth from before Him. A thousand thousands ministered to Him; ten thousand times ten thousand stood before Him. The court was seated, and the books were opened.*
>
> *Daniel 7:9-10*

We can learn a lot about the operation of a heavenly court by studying this passage accurately. First, we see that thrones are being put in place. A throne indicates a position of authority; it is a place where laws are established, a place of government and administration of justice. Decisions are made and orders are given.

But it is also a place where cases are judged. Verdicts are rendered, sometimes even death penalties. Laws are passed or revoked. Think about the State of the Union address when the President of the United States declares the policies of the government for the coming year. In the Netherlands, the king does this each year on the third Tuesday of

---

[38] Exodus 23::1-13
[39] Deuteronomy 10:18, 32:36; 1 Kings 8:49; Micah 7:9; Luke 18:1-9.

September in the Knight's Hall in The Hague. It is the only time when he actually sits on his throne.

Daniel doesn't see one throne in his vision, he sees more. It is a full court with multiple judges that together are qualified to render a verdict. We see, therefore, that the decision to take away the dominion of the beasts is taken by all judges; it is a joint decision.

Daniel sees someone coming who is described as *the Ancient of Days*. It is my opinion that this is the Almighty One, God the Judge, Creator of the heavens and the earth, the Eternal One. The throne of the Ancient of Days is different from the other thrones. There are flames of fire and there are wheels of burning fire carrying this throne. There is also a fiery river flowing from underneath this throne that goes before Him.

> *The Lord reigns; let the earth rejoice; let the multitude of isles be glad! Clouds and darkness surround Him; righteousness and justice are the foundation of His throne. A fire goes before Him and burns up His enemies round about.*
>
> *Psalm 97:1-3*

This is the throne where the Lord rules over His enemies. He judges in righteousness and justice and the verdicts are being executed by fire. Daniel then sees millions of beings that serve Him and hundreds of millions of witnesses before the throne. I imagine that we are also standing before His throne, not to be judged, but to see with our own eyes that the verdicts are being executed over *our* enemies.

> *I was watching in the night visions, and behold, one like the Son of Man, coming with the clouds of heaven! He came to the Ancient of Days, and they brought Him near before Him.*
> *Then to Him was given dominion and glory and a kingdom, that all peoples, nations, and languages should serve Him. His dominion is an everlasting dominion, which shall not pass away, and His kingdom the one which shall not be destroyed.*
>
> *Daniel 7:13-14*

Daniel describes, in this vision, one of the most important events in this creation. He tells us that one like the Son of Man is coming with the clouds of heaven and is brought before the Ancient of Days. I believe that Daniel is describing the ascension of Jesus as seen from heaven. After Jesus had fulfilled His destiny on the earth, He was brought before the throne of the

Ancient of Days. There He received the reward for the great effort He had delivered.

It is quite remarkable that Daniel sees an event in heaven that will take place on the earth six hundred years later. Our earthly dimension of time looks different in the heavenly dimensions. Daniel could see things that still needed to happen on the earth. What we see is that the honor that is given to Jesus is the result of a council decision that has been made in this courtroom. After all, we see that the court was in session and that the books were being opened. Everything that is being discussed here is based upon the things that were written in the books in heaven.

Jesus came to the earth because there was a scroll in which the will of God for His life was written.[40] When He appeared before the throne of the Ancient of Days, everything that He had done on the earth was judged based on what was written in the books.

The redemption of mankind could only take place if all the requirements of the Torah were fulfilled. The only institution that can judge if this is the case is the council of the Lord. I can only receive my salvation, my forgiveness of sin, my healing, and my restoration when there is a legal verdict. This is what Daniel is observing. Jesus is standing before the Judge of all and a verdict is rendered about everything He did on earth.

Did Jesus fulfill all the requirements of the Torah? Did He legally obtain the right to bring reconciliation for all the sins of humanity? Everything Jesus did on the earth, every conversation and thought, was written in the books in heaven. That is why the books are being opened because everything that is written therein is used as evidence in the court session.[41]

No wonder Daniel is being moved in the depths of his spirit when he observes this vision. He sees the restoration of the kingship, not only for the Son of God but for *all* the saints. The court that Daniel describes is a court that will justify *all* saints. This court has the jurisdiction to appoint kings and to dethrone them.

---

[40]   Hebrew 10:7, Psalm 139:16.
[41]   Revelations 20:12

Until the Ancient of Days came, and a judgment was made in favor of the saints of the Most High, and the time came for the saints to possess the kingdom.

Daniel 7:22

The book of Daniel describes the position Daniel had at the courts of the kings of Babylon. In his dialogues with King Nebuchadnezzar, only one question remained: Who has the real power on the earth? Daniel knew that there is a court in heaven and all the powers on the earth must obey it. What I find most interesting is that the name Daniel means: "God is my judge" or "judge of God." Is this the reason Daniel, above any other prophet, received such a deep understanding of the courts of heaven?

But the court shall be seated, and they shall take away his dominion, to consume and destroy it forever. Then the kingdom and dominion, and the greatness of the kingdoms under the whole heaven, shall be given to the people, the saints of the Most High. His kingdom is an everlasting kingdom, and all dominions shall serve and obey Him.

Daniel 7:26-27

This passage is talking about a court where verdicts are being rendered that have consequences for all life on the earth. I believe this is a description of the highest court in the kingdom of heaven. This court is called the Council of the Lord.

The Council of the Lord

In several passages, the Bible mentions a very special court called the Council of the Lord, also known as the congregation of the mighty.[42] Just as there are different kinds of government agencies and courts on the earth, there are also different kinds of governing bodies and courts in the heavenly dimension. However, there is one major difference between heaven and earth.

On earth, the judicial powers are in the hands of a fallen and corrupt government. As long as the kingdom of heaven hasn't been manifested in its full glory on the earth, corruption and abuse of power can still be present. That is why, in our society, the legislative, executive, and judicial

---

[42] Psalm 82

powers are separated. The power to govern is accommodated in different institutions. I will expand on this later.[43]

Perhaps you know the saying: *Power corrupts. Absolute power corrupts absolutely.* Although this might be true on earth, it is definitely not true in heaven.[44] God is called the Almighty One. Jesus has received *all* the power in heaven as on the earth. Yet both are far from corrupt. Their power is just and righteous. This is why the legislative, executive, and judicial powers can be in the hands of one court and even in the hands of one person.

The Hebrew word *sod* means "counsel, intimacy, and secret council." *Yasod* is Hebrew for the secret Council of the Lord. God as "Judge over all" gives His counselors, the sons of God, the opportunity to advise Him about His intentions before He makes a decision. This is a very important characteristic of our God. It is His desire that we are to be involved in the government of His kingdom. He wants to hear our opinion *before* He makes a decision. We can read about this in the book of Job, the Psalms, and Jeremiah.

> *Have you heard the counsel of God? Do you limit wisdom to yourself?*
> *Job 15:8*

> *For who has stood in the counsel of the Lord, and has perceived and heard His word? Who has marked His word and heard it?*
> *Jeremiah 23:18*

The decisions made in this *Yasod*—this Council of the Lord—impact the entire creation. More than that, the decisions that are made here are the foundation of our entire existence. After all, it is in this Council where the decision was made to create the human race in the image of the Creator.

> *Then God said, "Let Us make man in Our image, according to Our likeness; let them have dominion over the fish of the sea, over the birds of the air, and over the cattle, over all the earth and over every creeping thing that creeps on the earth.*
> *Genesis 1:26*

---

43 Page 64
44 Matthew 28:18

I was taught that "Let Us" in this verse refers to the triune God—the Father, Son, and Spirit. It was their decision to create the human race. But the Jewish interpretation sheds another light on this verse. The rabbis tell us that this verse is expressing the humbleness of our God.[45] Before He began to create the human race, He consulted with His board of advisors that were gathered together in a court setting. Much more can be told about this council, but that is outside the scope of this book. In a later chapter, I will go deeper into the decisions that are made in this council.[46]

The book of Amos shows us a different aspect of the Council of the Lord. This aspect has to do with the function that the prophets of God have in the kingdom of heaven. It is their task to speak the words on earth that the Supreme One has spoken in the *Yasod*. The prophets of the Lord are privileged to hear the counsel of the Lord in the *Yasod* and to pass them on.

> *Surely the Lord God does nothing, unless He reveals His secret to His servants the prophets. A lion has roared! Who will not fear? The Lord God has spoken! Who can but prophesy?*
>
> Amos 3:7-8

The word "secret" in this verse is the Hebrew word *sod*. In this place, God is sharing His secrets with His prophets. Now we shall see what words the prophet Micaiah heard in this Council.

The vision of Micaiah the prophet

Micaiah is a prophet that has been summoned to the gates of Samaria by the kings of Israel and Judah to advise them about state matters. In those days, it was customary for the prophets and seers to advise kings about important political and military decisions. This is one of the assignments of prophets. King Jehoshaphat and King Ahab were planning to go to war against the king of Syria in order to regain a piece of land.

All four hundred prophets of the court of King Ahab and Jezebel prophesied that the kings would be successful in battle. But King Jehoshaphat didn't trust them. He asked if there was another prophet, and so, Micaiah was summoned. The messenger tasked with bringing Micaiah to

---

45 *The Mystery of Creation according to Rashi*, Moznaim Publication Corporation, 1982.
46 Page 93

the kings told Micaiah what all the other prophets had prophesied, but Micaiah answered that he would only speak the words that the Lord had spoken to him.

Micaiah's first counsel to the kings matched the words of the other prophets, but King Ahab became furious. He knew that Micaiah tricked him. It was then that Micaiah told them what he really saw.

> Then Micaiah said, "Therefore hear the word of the Lord: I saw the Lord sitting on His throne, and all the host of heaven standing by, on His right hand and on His left. And the Lord said, 'Who will persuade Ahab to go up, that he may fall at Ramoth Gilead?' So one spoke in this manner, and another spoke in that manner. Then a spirit came forward and stood before the Lord, and said, 'I will persuade him.' The Lord said to him, 'In what way?' So he said, 'I will go out and be a lying spirit in the mouth of all his prophets.' And the Lord said, 'You shall persuade him, and also prevail. Go out and do so.'
>
> *1 Kings 22:19-22*

Here we see that the Lord is also making decisions that influence the earth from His throne. During this court session, the counselors are standing to the right and to the left side of the throne. The discussion is not a debate of deciding whether or not Ahab would die at Ramoth. No, their discussion is about the manner it will be executed.

Micaiah describes very precisely what he had observed in heaven. He paints a picture of the Almighty King asking for counsel concerning an important decision. Those who are in attendance are invited to present their ideas. Could it be that the things that are happening on earth are a real shadow of the things that are happening in heaven?

We see in Samaria that king Jehoshaphat and Ahab are also sitting on their thrones. They also ask for counsel about important state matters. We might conclude from this passage that the events on the earth are a shadow of the events in heaven. There are more scriptural references in the Bible where we see that what happens in heaven is also happening on the earth. This observation can help us tremendously, especially when we lack experience in observing what is going on in the spiritual dimension. When we study the situations on earth, we are able to form an idea of what is going on in heaven.

Things didn't end well for Micaiah. King Ahab said that Micaiah was to be thrown into prison until he, Ahab, safely returned from battle, proving that God hadn't spoken through Micaiah.

But King Ahab died and didn't return. Micaiah had spoken the truth. It is likely that this prophet spent the rest of his life in prison. The price that prophets of God pay for the honor to be an oracle on the earth for the Council of the Lord can be very high.

The Court Case of Job

Most people are familiar with the story of Job. He was a righteous and godly person who abruptly lost everything he owned and loved. And if that wasn't enough, he also became very ill and was cast out from his community. Many find comfort in the story of Job because in the end, all ended well.

But this is the story at the surface. There is much more going on in this book. In fact, the book of Job is the story of a legal suit between God and satan. From the beginning, we see this legal discussion going on between God and satan.

> *Now there was a day when the sons of God came to present them-*
> *selves before the Lord, and satan also came among them. And the*
> *Lord said to satan, "From where do you come?" So satan answered*
> *the Lord and said, "From going to and fro on the earth, and from*
> *walking back and forth on it." Then the Lord said to Satan, "Have you*
> *considered My servant Job, that there is none like him on the earth, a*
> *blameless and upright man, one who fears God and shuns evil?"*
> *So satan answered the Lord and said, "Does Job fear God for nothing?*
> *Have You not made a hedge around him, around his household, and*
> *around all that he has on every side? You have blessed the work of*
> *his hands, and his possessions have increased in the land. But now,*
> *stretch out Your hand and touch all that he has, and he will surely*
> *curse You to Your face!" And the Lord said to Satan, "Behold, all that*
> *he has is in your power; only do not lay a hand on his person." So*
> *satan went out from the presence of the Lord.*
>
> *Job 1:6-12*

Several things are happening here. First, the sons of God present them-selves before the throne. This wasn't a casual visit. When someone is presenting himself to a higher authority it is an official event, like when an ambassador presents his credentials to the king of the Netherlands. Then suddenly satan appears. Because the Lord asks him where he came from, it is clear that satan didn't present himself properly.

Now a legal discussion between the Judge and satan, the prosecutor, takes place concerning the life of Job. In it, we see that God highly praises Job because he is upright and blameless.

But satan says that he can't do anything to Job because there is a restraining order issued against him. There was a legal boundary around Job that made it impossible for satan to harm. But satan uses several arguments that give him the legal right to attack Job, and as a result, the Judge places Job and his possessions into the hands of satan.

But read carefully. Again, a legal restriction is put in place. Satan is not allowed to harm Job himself. There is a limit to the extent of satan's power. It appears the evil one doesn't have unlimited power. Rather, his actions are restrained by a legal cadre. The Judge has to give permission before satan is authorized to stretch out his hands against someone. Immediately after satan leaves the presence of the Lord, Job is overtaken by several disasters.

Sometime later, after Job loses all his children and numerous possessions, a second court session occurs. But this time, the sons of God are not the only ones that present themselves. Satan also presents himself and enters in an official capacity.

Again, there was a day when the sons of God came to present themselves before the Lord, and satan came also among them to present himself before the Lord. And the Lord said to Satan, "Behold, he is in your hand, but spare his life." So satan went out from the presence of the Lord and struck Job with painful boils from the sole of his foot to the crown of his head.

Job 2:1,6,7

During this session, satan obtains the legal right to attack Job personally. But again, he receives a restriction. He is not allowed to kill Job. Significant for both situations is the manner in which satan presents his arguments. He accuses God that he can't touch Job. This doesn't impress the Almighty One at all. God further praises Job, besides acknowledging that he still had a lot to learn.

Placing Boundary Stones

We read in both instances that satan doesn't have unlimited power to un-
leash his fiery wrath upon Job. The Judge puts a restriction on his power.
In the first case, satan is not allowed to touch Job; he may only harm his
family and his possessions. In the second session, satan is again con-
fronted with a restraining order. Now he can touch Job, but he is not allowed to kill him.

Satan is constantly searching for legal ground by which he can attack
us. He uses our own sins, the sins from our ancestors, or the sins of our
culture. At the moment he has obtained enough evidence, he will present
this evidence into court. There he will demand the right to hinder us and
stonewall us. This happened to the disciples of Jesus as well. Satan did
everything in order to destroy them.

> *Simon, Simon, satan has asked to sift each of you like wheat. But I*
> *have pleaded in prayer for you, Simon, that your faith should not fail.*
> *So when you have repented and turned to Me again, strengthen your*
> *brothers.*
>
> *Luke 22:31-32 (NLT)*

We often hear that satan was only attacking Peter, but Jesus states clearly
that satan had demanded to sift each of the disciples. Perhaps you are
asking why God allowed satan to sift them. Why didn't Jesus say that the
demands of satan were unlawful?

We must realize that what happened to Job and to the disciples was
allowed because there were legal grounds. But even so, everything ultimately worked to their advantage. The restrictions that Job experienced
in his walk with God were taken away. The disciples were purified from
the chaff that was in their lives. That is why Jesus tells them that when
they have repented, they should strengthen their brothers. God has all
power in the heavens and on the earth. Satan is not able to exceed Him.
Whatever happens in our lives, we can be sure that everything works for
the good for those who love Him.[47]

Jesus tells Simon that He has asked for a restriction, just as it was done
in the life of Job. Jesus asked that their faith might be preserved. Again,
the extent of satan's power was restricted. This is very important. Satan's

---

[47]   Romans 8:28

room for maneuvering is being restricted during the court case of Job. When we are approaching the courts of heaven to plead for ourselves, our family, or our city, we too can ask the Judge to restrict satan's room for maneuvering. This is an important part during the court session because we don't want to allow satan the freedom to do what he wants.

Again, the extent of satan's power was restricted.
This is very important.

This is an authority we can apply when we are interceding. Jesus said that in the last days there will be all kind of wars, earthquakes, and disasters.[48] But we are allowed to intercede before the throne and ask the Judge to limit the power of satan. It is not always possible to prevent earthquakes from happening, but you could ask that the strength is limited to a factor five on the Richter scale or that a hurricane will not exceed wind gusts above 80 mph. This is the way we take responsibility for the territory God has placed us in.

The Pleadings of Job

As I mentioned earlier, the book of Job is a description of a court session. There are many verses in Scripture that tell us a legal battle is going on. We see this in the use of words like *mediator, (in)justice, iniquity, righteousness, righteous, contend,* and *court case.* At some point, Job understood that there must be more to the story. What happened to him can't be a coincidence.

> *Listen carefully to my speech, and to my declaration with your ears. See now, I have prepared my case, I know that I shall be vindicated. Who is he who will contend with me? If now I hold my tongue, I perish.*
>
> *Job 13:17-19*

The word *declaration* could be seen as presenting a case in a court session. Job knows that more is going on, but he doesn't yet know who his adversaries are. He also hasn't a clue why this is happening to him. He

---

48   Matthew 24:7; Luke 21:9

doesn't know what charges are brought against him. That's why he is seeking solutions to make his complaint to be heard.

> *I would present my case before Him, and fill my mouth with arguments. I would know the words which He would answer me, and understand what He would say to me. Would He contend with me in His great power? No! But He would take note of me. There the upright could reason with Him, and I would be delivered forever from my Judge.*
>
> *Job 23:4-7*

How often do we experience the same struggle in our lives? Some great injustice has been done to us and deep inside we know that we are not to blame for it. Of course, we are not perfect, but the misery that is happening to us is not proportionate to the debts we owe God. In all this Job is not sinning with his words. He doesn't always speak words of wisdom, but he stays respectful and in awe of the Almighty God who is his Judge.

Finally, at the end of Job's ordeal, it is God Himself who appears to Job and rescues him out of his misery. For four chapters God, the Almighty One, is speaking with Job. I think this is the longest recorded speech from God in the Bible.

Notice the way in which God is helping Job. He asks him an endless string of questions to which Job does not have answers. But answers are not the point. These questions help Job to distance himself from his own circumstances. God brings him to the beginning of all things. He shows Job how his circumstances look when seen from the point of eternity, before God even began His creation. God helps Job to remember how things were at the beginning.

Job finally sees who his real adversary is and what has been done to him. He gets to know which charges were held against him. All this is described in the last chapters of Job's book. How does this battle end? Job surrenders himself to God and acknowledges that God is all-powerful. His eyes have finally seen the Almighty One. That brings an end to all discussion. This is what we can learn from Job: No matter how fierce the battle is, keep your eyes fixed on the One who can redeem us.

Therefore we also, since we are surrounded by so great a cloud of
witnesses, let us lay aside every weight, and the sin which so easily
ensnares us, and let us run with endurance the race that is set before
us, looking unto Jesus, the author and finisher of our faith, who for
the joy that was set before Him endured the cross, despising the
shame, and has sat down at the right hand of the throne of God.
Hebrews 12:1-2

The main purpose of the court case in the book of Job is to free him from the limitations in experiencing God as He really is. Although Job was righteous and just, he only knows the Almighty One from hearsay. This battle changed Job's heart. He became a humble person who could now say: "My eyes have seen You and I consider myself low."

Let this be an encouragement for us. In the end, God will reward us in the same manner as he has rewarded Job if we endure until the end.

For you have need of endurance, so that after you have done the will
of God, you may receive the promise: "For yet a little while, and He
who is coming will come and will not tarry. Now the just shall live by
faith; but if anyone draws back, My soul has no pleasure in him."
Hebrews 10:36-38

Conclusion

We have made a short journey through the Bible in this chapter. We have seen a few examples of the heavenly court systems. If you want to learn more about this, study the Psalms. David has written a lot about righteousness and justice. There are also other passages in Scripture that refer to the courts of heaven.

The government of God is founded on the heavenly court system. In essence, the kingdom of God is founded on righteousness and justice. These are the foundations of His throne and of His government. He is the Judge over all the earth, and He speaks justice over everything and everyone in His creation. Only when your eyes are opened to this truth are you able to see how often the Bible uses legal language.

In the next chapter, we will see that Jesus was charged in three different courts before they could sentence Him to death.

4

The Conviction of Jesus Christ

As we have seen before, the processes and protocols on earth are an indication of what happens in heaven. When we understand that there are several courts on earth, we can conclude that this will also be the case in heaven.

Every court on earth has its own jurisdiction and power to judge. Likewise, every court in heaven has its own jurisdiction and the power to render a verdict about certain situations. Just as there is the International Crime Court in the Hague, there is also such a court in heaven called the court of war.

When we look at the crucifixion of Jesus from a legal perspective, we see that He was interrogated in several different kinds of courts. In the end, Jesus was sentenced to death in *one* court; the other courts didn't have the jurisdiction to do so. To make this clear, I want to take you to Jerusalem to see how the trial of Jesus was conducted.

Jerusalem AD 33

The situation in Jerusalem is tense. More than 250,000 Jews are coming together in just a few square miles to celebrate Passover. They celebrate the deliverance of an enemy that held them captive and oppressed them for centuries. You can imagine that the Romans are on their guard. Judea is known as a rebellious province of the Roman Empire, which is why Caesar had sent the warhorse Pontius Pilate as governor to keep the peace. His display of power is also an expression of contempt, as if he's saying: "You can sing, dance, and pray as much as you like, but you are and always will be subjects of Rome." Pilate is known for the cruelty by which he carries out his orders.

The members of the Sanhedrin formed the religious council in Jewish society. This council consists of members of the Pharisees and Sadducees, and they were the highest religious court in Israel. The Romans were not at all interested in the internal legal affairs of the Jews. They wanted one thing—peace in the region. This gave the leaders of the Jewish people some room to maneuver, but they knew very well that they would be held personally accountable if things got out of hand. It would cost them their lives in the cruelest sense of the word.

In the last few years, the popularity of Jesus has become so huge that it becomes a problem for the members of the council. The straw that breaks the camel's back is the resurrection of Lazarus. Many Jews come to realize that this Jesus is more than just a carpenter. They start to believe that He could be the promised Messiah who will restore the kingdom of David. In the meantime, He will also deal with the Romans. That is why the chief priests and the Pharisees are calling the council together; they are to make a decision about His death.

Then the chief priests and the Pharisees gathered a council and said, "What shall we do? For this Man works many signs. If we let Him alone like this, everyone will believe in Him, and the Romans will come and take away both our place and nation."

John 11:47-48

During Passover, the religious leaders have a massive and complex problem: 250,000 believers gathered in a crowded city, a Messiah who has become a popular hero, and Roman authorities that are suspiciously monitoring it all. This alone is enough reason to capture Jesus before the celebration of Passover.

But their greatest nightmare becomes a reality when Jesus enters the east gate and the people start to cheer Him as King. It is vital for them to nip this movement in the bud. Whether Jesus must die or not is no longer a question for them. Be it out of jealousy or conviction, they conclude that the death of Jesus is necessary to maintain the peace in Judea and to save their own lives. The only question remaining is how to legally accomplish this. They can't simply commit an assault on His life; that would start an enormous rebellion. No, they must convince the people that His death, based on Torah, is justified.

And the chief priests and the scribes sought how they might kill Him, for they feared the people.

Luke 22:2

For the first time, they are having some luck. Judas volunteers to help them arrest Jesus. Jesus is arrested in the garden of Gethsemane and interrogated in the inner court of Caiaphas' palace. They try to press charges and bring conclusive evidence into court in order to close the case. But a court case is established on the testimony of two or three witnesses, so they bribe witnesses to give false statements. This breaks the law of Moses, but the goal justifies the means, doesn't it?[49]

Despite all their efforts, they're not able to present their evidence so that it is legally conclusive. Just as they are getting desperate, Jesus Himself meets them halfway. His testimony is so powerful that they don't need any other witnesses.

> *And the high priest arose and said to Him, "Do You answer nothing? What is it these men testify against You?" But Jesus kept silent. And the high priest answered and said to Him, "I put You under oath by the living God: Tell us if You are the Christ, the Son of God!" Jesus said to him, "It is as you said. Nevertheless, I say to you, hereafter you will see the Son of Man sitting at the right hand of the Power and coming on the clouds of heaven." Then the high priest tore his clothes, saying, "He has spoken blasphemy! What further need do we have of witnesses? Look, now you have heard His blasphemy! What do you think?" They answered and said, "He is deserving of death."*
> *Matthew 26:62-66*

If Jesus would have remained silent, it is my conviction that the council could never have condemned Him to death. But now it is Jesus that presents the evidence needed. He is found guilty of the charges and, according to Jewish law, needs to die. The problem is that the Jewish leaders, who are subjected to Roman government, have no jurisdiction to carry out the death penalty.

The Sanhedrin

The conviction of Jesus starts with the interrogation in the religious court—the Sanhedrin. Jesus is judged here based on the Jewish religious laws. The Sanhedrin is composed of seventy members and is presided by the High Priest of that year, Caiaphas. This council has the jurisdiction to

---

[49]   Exodus 23:1-13

condemn someone to the death penalty, but they are not allowed to execute it under the Roman government.

In Acts 5, we see an interesting story of how the Sanhedrin operates.
After the pouring out of the Holy Spirit, everything went completely
wrong for them. The once-small group of followers of Jesus became a
growing, influential movement, and the crowds loved them. Killing Jesus
didn't give the Sanhedrin the desired outcome. So, they tried by any
means possible to prevent this movement from gaining momentum. They
arrested the leaders, interrogated them, and punished them. The Sanhedrin was authorized to do this, or the people would have rebelled against
them. But thanks to the counsel of Gamaliel, the believers were not condemned to death. They were just beaten and set free.

That is why they pressed charges against Jesus
that are based upon Roman law.

Afterward, we see that Saul received letters from the Sanhedrin that gave
him extensive powers. His authority was based upon the council decision
that the Sanhedrin took and wrote on a scroll. This council decision gave
him the mandate to hunt for Jews who had converted into followers of
Jesus. The jurisdiction of the Sanhedrin was so far-reaching that Saul was
even authorized to capture Jews in a foreign nation.

*Then Saul, still breathing threats and murder against the disciples of
the Lord, went to the high priest and asked letters from him to the
synagogues of Damascus, so that if he found any who were of the
Way, whether men or women, he might bring them bound to Jerusalem.*

Acts 9:1-2

Pilate's Court

After the conviction of Jesus by the leaders of the Sanhedrin, they take
Him to the court of Pilate. Pilate isn't at all interested in the internal problems of the Jews. That's why he says: "Judge Him according to your law."

They answered and said to him, "If He were not an evildoer, we would not have delivered Him up to you." Then Pilate said to them, "You take Him and judge Him according to your law." Therefore, the Jews said to him, "It is not lawful for us to put anyone to death."

John 18:30-31

Pilate doesn't want a revolt in a crowded city, but the chief priests and the scribes aren't dismissed that easily. They are determined to execute Jesus before the start of Passover. That is why they press charges against Jesus that are based upon Roman law. Pilate grows more cornered by the minute. Does he really need to judge this man? He doesn't want to do that at all. His assignment is to keep the peace in Judea. He grows concerned that killing a national hero will not lend stability or peace in the region.

This is why Pilate asks exactly what charges have been brought against Jesus. The accusations the Jews have brought are not about the eternal salvation that Jesus promises to all who believe in Him; they are not about taking care of the poor or serving God with all your heart. Instead, they bring accusations against Jesus based on violations of Roman law.

Pilate then went out to them and said, "What accusation do you bring against this Man?"

John 18:29

The Jews charge that Jesus has claimed He is the Son of God and that He will lead an inevitable rebellion against Caesar. According to Roman law, there can only be *one* god: Caesar, who self-proclaimed himself the son of god and the king of all kings. Everyone subject to the Roman government must honor him.

The Jews charge that Jesus has claimed He is the Son of God and would lead an inevitable rebellion against Caesar.

Under Roman law, the title of "son of god" belongs only to one person: Caesar. The coins of his empire even state this. As soon as Pilate hears that Jesus calls Himself the Son of God and is honored as King by the Jewish people, he is terrified. As governor from Judea, he has the authority to declare the death penalty. Roman law gave him this jurisdiction.

The Court of Herod

As soon as the opportunity presents itself to have Jesus convicted else-where, Pilate takes it. He sends Jesus to the court of Herod. This court is authorized to render a verdict over *all* Galileans. Perhaps Pilate thought he could pull a trick on Herod; these two men were enemies of each other. Or maybe Pilate thought: *Let Herod deal with it. I will dodge this bullet.*

> *And as soon as he knew that He belonged to Herod's jurisdiction, he sent Him to Herod, who was also in Jerusalem at that time.*
>
> Luke 23:7

Although Herod is authorized to judge Galileans, he fails to render a ver-dict. When Jesus appears before Herod, He doesn't say a word, making it impossible for Herod to convict Him. This is surprising and notable be-cause Jesus answers questions at the Sanhedrin and in the court of Pilate. It seems to me that Jesus is indicating that he doesn't recognize the court of Herod.

The Conviction

But soon the charade is over. Herod sends Jesus back to Pilate, wrapped in a gorgeous robe. Like Joseph, Jesus is handed over by his brothers to a foreign power. It is also worth mentioning that Pilate and Herod become friends through these events.

Jesus is transported from one court to another, all in the effort to have Him legally convicted to death. The chief priests and Pharisees are get-ting desperate. The great Shabbat was nearly upon them. They must hurry. Jesus has to be killed before sunset, one way or another. The chief priests and Pharisees urge Pilate to condemn Jesus to the death penalty.

Pilate tries to avoid the conviction of Jesus three times. He can't find anything Jesus has done that deserves the death penalty. But the leaders of the Jewish nation begin a revolt there in the court, which is exactly what Pilate doesn't want, so he surrenders Jesus to be crucified.

> *Then he said to them the third time, "Why, what evil has he done? I have found no reason for death in Him. I will therefore chastise Him and let Him go." But they were insistent, demanding with loud voices that He be crucified.*

And the voices of these men and of the chief priests prevailed. So Pilate gave sentence that it should be as they requested. And he released to them the one they requested, who for rebellion and murder had been thrown into prison; but he delivered Jesus to their will.

Luke 23:22-24

Conclusion

The crucifixion of Jesus was an event that strikes us deep in our hearts. Our salvation, restoration, and freedom have been obtained at the cross. It was very important that His suffering and death met all legal requirements. The victory over satan was endorsed by the legal verdict that the Judge over all the earth rendered. Because satan was legally defeated, we are legally justified from sin.

We see that every legal party in Jesus' trial was bound by the rules and regulations of their own legal system. The chief priests and Pharisees convicted Jesus based on Torah. The trial before Herod was a charade. He couldn't get the conviction because of a lack of evidence. Pilate only convicted Jesus based upon Roman law, as those charges had to meet the requirements of that law.

These lessons are very important to us. When injustice has been done to us and we want to be vindicated by God, we must not only comply with the legal protocols. We must also approach the right court. If we don't do that, our adversary could declare us inadmissible. This can also happen if our charges are not based on the proper law. Only when we appear in the proper court and our charges are based upon the proper laws is God able to acquit us.

Let us, therefore, discover in which court we must present our case. There is a court where every believer, based on the Word of God, may present his case. This court is called the mobile court and will be discussed in the next chapter.

5

The Mobile Court

The Government in The Kingdom

There are many stories in the Bible where we can see a glimpse of what is going on in heaven. Abraham, Moses, David, Paul, John, and many prophets saw or experienced the activities of heaven, and these experiences were written down for *us*. Drawing from these passages about the governmental structures in heaven, many civilizations on the earth have set up similar structures that are a shadow of heavenly governmental structures.

In the Bible, the word "government" is used three times. The most familiar passage is Isaiah 9:6-7, where the prophecy about Jesus states that *the government shall be on His shoulders*. This passage not only speaks of an earthly government but also refers to the heavenly government. On earth, a governor rules over a certain territory and has dominion over it. His government is based upon the laws of that country and those laws specify the extent of his power.

The best way to understand heavenly government is to study the concepts in ancient Israel. The synagogue formed the essence of Jewish society. It was the central place for meeting one another. It was a place to pray, to learn, and to speak justice. The Beth Din, also called "house of judges" or the "bench of three" formed the leadership of a synagogue.[50] This council consisted of a minimum of three members. To be a member of this council, it was expected that one be well grounded in the Torah and lead a righteous life.

Seven righteous and respected men and women supported the Beth Din, and they were called the "bench of seven." The members of this combined team of ten people led the synagogue. They were exempt from any labor. In this way, they could focus on studying the Torah and supporting the community. They provided education, met pastoral needs, and spoke

---

50 Wikipedia: https://en.wikipedia.org/wiki/Beth_din.

justice in the village. A synagogue could only be established when the community was able to support this team of ten leaders.

Biblical Examples of a Beth Din

The Bible shows us many examples of a Beth Din in function. This is a team of three persons that is responsible for the government of its domain. The people of Israel have three founding fathers: Abraham, Isaac, and Jacob. Noah, who governed the new earth, had three sons: Shem, Cham, and Japhet. David governed his kingdom with three heroes: Josheb-Basshebeth, Eleazar, and Shammah. Daniel was supported in Babylon by his friends Hananiah, Mishael, and Azariah. Jesus had three disciples that formed His inner circle: John, Peter, and James.

The members of the Beth Din had the jurisdiction to legislate rules and regulations and had dominion in the spiritual dimension. This is what Jesus was talking about when He spoke about binding and loosing on earth. What they decided on earth had consequences in heaven.

And I will give you the keys of the kingdom of heaven, and whatever you bind on earth will be bound in heaven, and whatever you loose on earth will be loosed in heaven.
Matthew 16:19

We see in our society a clear example of this type of government. Every earthly government is a shadow of a heavenly structure. Many nations are familiar with the concept of separation of powers, also known as the trias politica. Under this model, a state's government is divided into branches, each with separate and independent powers and areas of responsibility, so that the powers of one branch are not in conflict with the powers associated with the other branches. The typical division is three branches: a legislature, an executive, and a judiciary, which is the trias politica model.[51]

The legislature power makes the laws to govern the nation. The executive power is responsible for the daily governance of the nation, like the police forces or the armed forces. The judiciary powers are responsible for testing this execution according to the law.

---

[51] https://en.wikipedia.org/wiki/Separation_of_powers

A different form of the bench of three can be seen in the sporting world. In many sports there are three winners that are set above the other contestants. They rule over them and are rewarded with gold, silver, and bronze as a token of their supremacy over the others. Most athletes aim to be in the top ten of their game.

The Government in Heaven

In heaven, the government of the throne of God is also called the Beth Din, or Bench of Three. This government is in the hands of God the Father, God the Son, and God the Holy Spirit. They are superior above everything that is created. The seven spirits of God that stand before the throne support the government of the triune God. Ian Clayton explains in his book that the seven spirits of God support the throne and are not an expression of the Holy Spirit.[52]

According to Rabbi Dr. Hillel ben David, Paul refers to the operation of this bench of seven in the synagogue in Ephesians 4.[53] This bench was comprised of an apostle, a prophet, an evangelist, three pastors, and a teacher.[54] Their task was to equip the saints to mature them in Christ. While the leaders of the Beth Din were in charge of the synagogue, they were not visible. They were hidden in Christ inside the menorah. They were responsible for education, prayer, and speaking justice. The seven helpers were responsible for the pastoral care and the wellbeing of their community. Together they were the Light of Christ. They were the menorah; the light that shines into the world.

We find another great example of this support in Acts. When the Greek-speaking Jews were neglected in the daily distribution, a tense situation began to simmer among the members of the first church. The apostles gathered under the leadership of Peter, John, and James to discuss this matter. They decided to appoint seven wise and godly men who would be charged with the responsibility for the pastoral care of the church. The apostles devoted themselves to prayer and ministering the word.

---

[52] Realms of the Kingdom part 1, published by Seraph Creative in 2014.
[53] http://www.betemunah.org/synagog.html
[54] Ephesians 4:11-13

Therefore, brethren, seek out from among you seven men of good reputation, full of the Holy Spirit and wisdom, whom we may appoint over this business; but we will give ourselves continually to prayer and to the ministry of the word.

Acts 6:3-4

When we are presenting our case in the courts of heaven, we need heavenly advisors and supporters. These are, among others, the seven Spirits of God. They will help us during the court proceedings. They are the eyes of the Lord that run to and fro throughout the whole earth on behalf of those whose hearts are loyal to Him.[55] They are being presented to us in Isaiah 11.

The Spirit of the Lord shall rest upon Him, The Spirit of wisdom and understanding, The Spirit of counsel and might, The Spirit of knowledge and of the fear of the Lord.

Isaiah 11:2

When we are presenting our case in the courts of heaven, we need heavenly advisors and supporters.

We need Wisdom and Revelation for the preparation of our case. We need Counsel to prepare our pleadings in the right way. We need the Knowledge and the Fear of the Lord to act with honor and respect during the court session. We need Strength and Might to execute the verdicts upon the earth. We need the Spirit of the Lord to be confirmed in our office and position. Without the support of the seven Spirits of the Lord, operating in the courts of heaven will be much more difficult.

The Counsel of Jethro

When you are part of a synagogue and a minor dispute arises, one must first go to the Beth Din—the house of judges. This is still true today. You present your case before the leaders of your local synagogue. More important or complex cases are referred to higher courts. Every tribe in Israel had a judicial body; this council had 23 members. The highest council in Israel was located in Jerusalem and was called the Sanhedrin.

---

[55] 2 Chronicles 16:9

This classification is based upon the counsel of Jethro; the father-in-law of Moses. While Moses was judging the people of Israel, those with disputes were standing and waiting for their turn to appear before him. Jethro observed this and concluded that Moses would be unable to do this job single-handedly. He advised Moses to share the responsibilities among just and righteous men.

> *Moreover, you shall select from all the people able men, such as fear God, men of truth, hating covetousness; and place such over them to be rulers of thousands, rulers of hundreds, rulers of fifties, and rulers of tens. And let them judge the people at all times. Then it will be that every great matter they shall bring to you, but every small matter they themselves shall judge. So it will be easier for you, for they will bear the burden with you. If you do this thing, and God so commands you, then you will be able to endure, and all this people will also go to their place in peace.*
>
> *Exodus 18:21-23*

Moses listened to the counsel of Jethro and chose able men, appointing them as judges over the people. They judged the small cases; larger matters were referred to Moses.

This is still a valid principle. In the Netherlands, special courts are established to judge the matters that are part of everyday life. These matters could be about labor disputes, conflicts between neighbors, or matters that have a low financial significance. These courts are formally known as a municipal court. They still exist in the Netherlands as a special branch of the court system. They are decentralized departments of the court.

There are more municipal courts than regular courts. In terms of distance, these municipal courts are easier to approach. It is not difficult to personally present your case, even without the aid of a lawyer. This is a court with a low threshold. For other cases (usually those that are more difficult or have a greater interest), you need to go to a regular court. There are fewer of these courts and the threshold to approach them is much higher.

It is far more difficult to present your case in a regular court. You can't approach a regular court without the assistance of a lawyer. The judicial complexity of a regular court makes it mandatory that a lawyer assists you. Therefore, it is important that you present your case to the right court and judge. When you approach a municipal court with a complex case, the judge will decline jurisdiction and refer you to a higher court.

The Mobile Court

The simplest way to gain understanding of the courts of heaven is to examine the differences between central and mobile courts. Central courts are in a fixed position in one of the spiritual dimensions. The mobile court is more easily accessible to us. It is in session on earth anywhere the Judge opens the court.

During my study of the courts of heaven, I found an interesting article about the ancient constitution of the British Empire.[56] This constitution had an advisory and legislative council. This council presided in London and made decisions about important state matters. The council was called the *King's Council* (Latin: *Curia Regis*). The council was in session whenever the king ordered it to be so.

When the king traveled through his domain, counselors, and officers of the court always accompanied him. The subjects of the king could approach him and personally present their cases before him. The king could open the court on site and render a verdict. This is a great example of the way the mobile court operates. The king leaves his palace and comes to his subjects to render a verdict on site.

In the Netherlands, it is possible that a judge will go to the people to look into a situation personally. Officially this is called a *descentee* (French for descending). The judge steps down from his judgment seat to do an on-location examination of the case that is being presented to him. We have a Dutch television show called *The Traveling Judge*.[57] It is legally permissible for a judge to make binding decisions outside the official protocol of a courtroom, though this is only possible if all parties agree to it. It may happen that the traveling judge can render a verdict in a bar in Montana, or solve a neighborly quarrel in Hemet, California. The mobile court comes to the people.

---

[56] https://en.wikipedia.org/wiki/Curia_regis
[57] https://rijdenderechter.kro-ncrv.nl/over-de-rijdende-rechter

The Intercession of Abraham

Something like a mobile court happened to Abraham. He was visited by three men (perhaps a Beth Din from heaven) by whom the Lord shared with Abraham what He had decided about the destruction of Sodom and Gomorrah.

There are some very interesting things happening here. First of all, God said that the outcry about Sodom and Gomorrah was great. Their sins were brought before His presence. The accusations against these cities were not spoken on the earth, but in the heavenly realm. It was there that God heard what was going on in Sodom and Gomorrah. The Bible then described the Lord going to Sodom and Gomorrah to investigate for Himself. He wanted to know if the accusations were true or not.

I will go down now and see whether they have done altogether according to the outcry against it that has come to Me; and if not, I will know.

Genesis 18:21

Another interesting note is that Abraham began to intercede, and he applied the Beth Din rules. A city would only be recognized in heaven when there were ten righteous people who could represent her—the Beth Din of three persons and the bench of seven. When a city didn't support ten people to carry the responsibility to serve the city, this city didn't have the mandate to plead in the courts of heaven.

Do we now understand why Abraham, while he was interceding for Sodom and Gomorrah, stopped at ten righteous men? Abraham was talking to God in His formal capacity as Judge over all the earth. He knew that the very existence of these cities was at stake. He was interceding before the Judge of the whole earth in an attempt to save them.

Far be it from You to do such a thing as this, to slay the righteous with the wicked, so that the righteous should be as the wicked; far be it from You! Shall not the Judge of all the earth do right?

Genesis 18:25

But there is one major problem. No Beth Din was assigned in these cities, so Abraham couldn't do anything for these cities. He was not mandated to intercede in the mobile court for these cities; the citizens of these cities were responsible to do this themselves. Both cities were destroyed, and the soil remains infertile to this day. This story is a very clear biblical example of the operation of a mobile court. God Himself came down to render a verdict on the earth and He invited His friends to intercede there.

To intercede for the salvation of a city, it must have a government that is recognized in heaven.

In our time, the same principle applies. To intercede for the salvation of a city, it must have a government that is recognized in heaven. When ten righteous people come together to stand in the gap for their nation, they form an ecclesia together that is recognized in heaven. The prayer of *this* ecclesia will be heard in the courts of heaven. Their intercession carries a lot of weight when the verdict is being rendered for a city, a region, or a nation.

Entering the Mobile Court

According to the Jews, heaven is not far away. To them, it is a dimension that surrounds them. Jesus started His ministry by proclaiming the kingdom of God is at hand.[58] Heaven is as close as the warmth that I feel coming from my hand when I hold it next to my face. Try this and you'll see what I mean.

We have been taught that heaven is always above us, so we point to the sky when we talk about heavenly matters. But someone from New Zealand is doing the same and they point in exactly the opposite direction. What is above for them is beneath for us.

In short, the heavenly dimension is not above or beneath us; it is *around* us. We can go through the veil, entering this dimension by faith. The invitation is clear, as are the desires of our Father. He looks forward to seeing us in His dimension.

---

[58] Matthew 3:2; Mark 1:15; Luke 21:31

Therefore, brethren, having boldness to enter the Holiest by the blood of Jesus, by a new and living way which He consecrated for us, through the veil, that is, His flesh, and having a High Priest over the house of God, let us draw near with a true heart in full assurance of faith, having our hearts sprinkled from an evil conscience and our bodies washed with pure water. Let us hold fast the confession of our hope without wavering, for He who promised is faithful.

Hebrews 10:19-23

For years I have wrestled with this passage. How do I enter the Holiest? I desperately longed to experience this. I discovered there was a complete chapter written about walking in faith after this passage. It was then I understood that entering the heavenly dimensions is an act of faith. We need faith because without faith it is not possible to approach Him or see Him. The way is open through the blood of Jesus and through His body. This is a clear reference to the Lord's Supper. When we have communion regularly, such as once each day, we can experience the heavenly dimensions more easily.

The same is true for entering the mobile court. We enter by faith in the conviction that He will hear us. I am convinced that we have entered the mobile court without being conscious of it. Every time we cry out to God to justify us, we are actually in this mobile court.

It is important to understand that entering this court is an act we do first in our spirit. We were created by God as a triune being. We are a spiritual being by birth from heaven, our soul is redeemed and renewed, and our body is the temple of the Holy Spirit.[59] God created this trinity after His own image. We experience and encounter the spiritual dimension under the authority of our spirit. In Chapter Nine, I will explain why we need the prophetic gifting in order to be able to operate properly in the courts of heaven.

We read in the story of Sodom and Gomorrah that God came down to the earth in order to render a verdict. Similarly, when He approaches us, the mobile court is in session. He comes to us because we are approaching Him.[60] Perhaps we are not able to see Him, but He is right there. And

---

[59] 1 Thessalonians 5:23
[60] James 4:8

just as we approach God in faith, knowing that He exists, we can also enter this mobile court. We enter by faith into this spiritual dimension.

It is a simple matter of being absolutely sure that this court exists and that we have the mandate to present our case there. The first steps are always the most difficult because we have no frame of reference. We have not yet experienced it as real.

But we have been invited to enter in, to let our voice be heard in heaven, and to present our case before Him. When we enter step-by-step, we will experience confirmation. That is how our frame of reference is being formed—through experience. This is also the starting point for the next step. The purpose of this book is to assist you to grow in sonship by taking up the responsibilities of a mature son[61] in manifesting this kingdom of heaven on the earth. When we do, wherever we go, His will is done on earth as it is in heaven.

The Throne of Grace

A final comment. There is a difference between the throne of grace and the mobile court. They have different objectives. We enter the court because injustice has been done to us and we want to be justified. But we go to the throne of grace to receive mercy and grace.

> *Let us therefore come boldly to the throne of grace, that we may obtain mercy and find grace to help in time of need.*
>
> *Hebrews 4:16*

The Dutch translation of this passage tells us that we receive our help at the right time. But in the English translation, it says that we receive it at the time of our need. That is exactly the difference between the throne of grace and the mobile court. In the mobile court, a verdict will be rendered because of the injustice that has been done to us; acts that were meant to destroy the plan and destiny God has for us. It is His desire that we are to

---

[61] Jesus explains in Scripture that in heaven the distinction between male and female doesn't exist. But it clearly tells us that as sons we receive the authority to rule as kings. We have transcended the gender we had on the earth. We are all sons of God, like Jesus is.

be successful in the realization of our destinies. These destinies are written out in our scroll and ratified by a council decision.

But when we approach the throne of grace, we can share our grief and our sorrow with God our Father. Our tears are collected there and are wiped away from our eyes.[62] It has a different purpose.

Conclusion

We have seen that there are several different courts on the earth and they each have their specific jurisdiction. It is important for us to know that there is a spiritual court that we can approach from the earth. We can present our cases there and ask to be vindicated. This court is called the mobile court and we enter it from the earth by faith.

We need to step in faith. The spiritual dimension is around us and Christ has prepared the way for us to enter it. When we approach Him, He will approach us in His capacity as Judge. Like the ancient king of England and the traveling judge in the Netherlands, He will render a verdict on the place where we have set our foot. He gives us the opportunity to present our personal cases before Him.

Many earthly courts deal with disputes over contracts or broken agreements such as legal contracts or tenancy agreements. The same is true in the courts of heaven. Covenants play an important legal role in these courts. In the next chapter, I will discuss the legal backgrounds of a covenant and their importance.

---

[62] Revelations 7:17

6

The Covenant: A Legal Contract

A covenant is a legal contract between two or more parties. It is a mutual agreement you are obligated to honor. When you make a covenant, you are actually signing a contract. Both parties agree to the obligations and the rights each will have. When they sign the contract, they state that they will meet the terms that are laid out in the contract. Witnesses are present that co-sign the contract. The documents, the signatures, and the witnesses enforce the covenant. When a covenant is sealed with blood, the legal force of it is stronger in heaven as well on earth.

The Hebrew word for covenant is *berith*, which means "to cut in half." That is the way by which covenants were made in the Old Testament. We read this in Genesis 15:7-21, where Abram killed several animals, cut them in pieces and divided the pieces. Both parties of the covenant stood opposite the other and swore an oath. In this manner, they promised that they would keep the covenant. Then they ratified the covenant by passing through the pieces of the sacrificed animals.

> *So he said to him, "Bring Me a three-year-old heifer, a three-year-old female goat, a three-year-old ram, a turtledove, and a young pigeon." Then he brought all these to him and cut them in two, down the middle, and placed each piece opposite the other; but he did not cut the birds in two.*
> *And it came to pass, when the sun went down and it was dark, that behold, there appeared a smoking oven and a burning torch that passed between those pieces.*
>
> *Genesis 15:9,10,17*

In Hebrews 9, we read about the deeper background of a covenant. We see that the covenants that God made with the people of Israel were consecrated with blood, and all objects in the tabernacle were purged with blood. The moment the priests brought their sacrifices to the tabernacle on earth, the sins of the people were blotted out in the courts of heaven.

And almost all things are by the law purged with blood; and without shedding of blood is no remission.

Hebrews 9:22

The writers of the book to the Hebrews explained that the power of the blood of calves and goats was limited. This blood could only remit the sins of Israel for one year. The sacrifice of the blood of Jesus, on the other hand, is so powerful that we receive an eternal redemption.[63]

A covenant that is ratified by blood has a much stronger voice in the courts of heaven. That is why satan tries to make blood covenants with individuals, cities, and nations. When blood is being shed, the terms of the covenant are sealed as well.

This doesn't mean that verbal commitments are without obligation. James tells us that our "yes" should mean "yes indeed."

But above all things, my brethren, swear not, neither by heaven, neither by the earth, neither by any other oath: but let your yea be yea; and your nay, nay; lest ye fall into condemnation.

James 5:12

When we make a promise and we don't follow up on that promise, that person can bring accusations against us. This is the warning James is giving us. Even Solomon advises us to take care to keep the verbal promises we made to God.[64] Be cautious in making casual promises because we can be held accountable for them. Every word that we speak and every thought that we have is recorded in heaven. David models this awareness in asking that the words of his mouth and the meditation of his heart be acceptable in God's sight.[65]

The Marriage Covenant

We can find many different kinds of covenants in the Bible. We see examples of covenants made between people, between tribes, and between nations. There are even covenants where the Lord is present as a witness.[66]

---

[63] Hebrews 9:12
[64] Ecclesiastes 5:3-6
[65] Psalm 19:14-15
[66] Genesis 21:32; 1 Samuel 11: 1; Joshua 9:6,15; Genesis 31:10

An important biblical covenant is the agreement made between man and wife called marriage. There are five different stages in the Jewish wedding traditions that lead up to a marriage. One key moment is when the man and woman draw up a contract, which happens during the third stage of the wedding preparations. During this stage, the negotiations take place about the content of the contract. The Hebrew word for this contract is called *ketubah*.

When they draw up the contract, both parents play an important role. They know their child much better than the child does. The parents are the official witnesses of this covenant. During these negotiations, the expectations of both partners are expressed based upon their equivalence. For example, they discuss how many children they would like, how much money the woman will receive for housekeeping, how possessions will be distributed between them, how often they will have sexual intercourse, and so forth. This ketubah is a protection for the woman in case the husband should send her away. The ketubah entails the rights and obligations of their marriage. If both parties keep their side of this ketubah, there is no legal ground for a divorce.

After the signing of the ketubah, the couple is formally married. The bride is allowed to carry the name of her husband and is entitled to do business on behalf of her husband. At this point, they do not have sexual intercourse. A time of preparation begins lasting about two to three years, in which the groom prepares a home for them. He lives in his father's house while he readies his newlywed home.

Mary was pregnant without the input of Joseph. This occurred before Joseph had built their home. This was a direct violation of the ketubah, which entitled Joseph to approach the Beth Din of his synagogue and ask them to dissolve the marriage contract. According to their ketubah, this couple was formally married. The contract had been signed. It speaks highly of Joseph's character that he wanted to do this quietly, without too much disclosure.[67]

When we study the book of Exodus from this marriage context, you'll find all five stages of the wedding ceremony.[68] The Jews do not view the Ten Commandments as a set of rules and obligations. They see them

---

[67] Matthew 1:19-20
[68] More can be found in Wake Up! Published by Het Zoeklicht, 2014

much more as a ketubah, a covenant contract between God and His people. They even call this passage in Scripture "the ten words of God." They are not mere commandments; they are the legal agreement between two equal partners. The stone tablets that contain these ten words are called the "Tablets of the Testimony." They were preserved in the "Ark of the Testimony."

The Power of Law of a Covenant

When we make a covenant, we are obligated to respect the agreement we made, even if we later discover that we have been double-crossed by the other party. We see a great example of this in Joshua 9. As the Israelites entered the Promised Land under the leadership of Joshua and began to overwhelmingly conquer, every king in that land panicked. They saw how Joshua dealt with Jericho and Ai and they feared for their lives.

Therefore, the citizens of Gibeon devised a scheme to seduce Joshua. They put on very old clothes, carried supplies of moldy bread, and went on a journey to meet Joshua. When they arrived, they praised and honored him for everything that God had done through him. You have to admit these men were very brave.

At first, the Israelites were on guard. "Why should we make a covenant with you?" they asked. "You might be living right in this land among us."

"No, no," the Gibeonites said. "Look at our food and our wineskins. The food was fresh, and the wineskins were new when we left home. Look, now our bread has molded, and the wineskins are gone."

The Israelites believed the lies of the Gibeonites, so Joshua and the men of Israel made a covenant with them. In doing so, they made one big mistake. They forgot to take counsel from the Lord and were deceived by the appearance of the Gibeonites and the fine words they used.

So Joshua made peace with them, and made a covenant with them to let them live; and the rulers of the congregation swore to them.
Joshua 9:15

You would be wise to be alert when people come to you and want to make a deal with you. Many times, this happens right after your first major successes. Any deal you make has legal power in heaven, even if the other party is lying to you. Psalm 15 says that we may live with God when we walk uprightly and work in righteousness. David tells us that we can't change our oath even if we experience the negative consequences of this oath.[69]

The covenant made with the Gibeonites was legal in heaven. When the Israelites realized three days later that they had been double-crossed, they were bound by the agreement they had made because they swore to the Lord, the God of Israel. Joshua was so furious at the Gibeonites that he cursed them and made them woodcutters and water carriers for the Israelite congregation for the rest of their lives.

Not long after, the five kings of the Amorites attacked the Gibeonites, who in turn sent a messenger to Joshua and called for help, invoking the covenant they had made with Israel. Joshua was obliged to come to their aid. He defeated the five kings of the Amorites with a great display of power. Even the sun and the moon fought with Joshua to give him the victory. This victory is a direct consequence of Joshua's decision to honor the covenant he made with the Gibeonites. Not only God, but the whole of heaven was behind Israel in this battle.

When Joshua made the covenant with the Gibeonites, this agreement was not merely valid for him and the leaders of the people of that time. Because he was a leader over Israel ordained by God, the covenant had legal power over all inhabitants of the nation of Israel. Even after Joshua died, this covenant still carried legal power. It was still valid when, approximately 500 years later, a great famine occurred in Israel during the reign of King David. For three years the earth did not bring forth fruit. David took counsel from the Lord asking for the cause of the famine. The answer he received was astonishing: Bloodshed rested on the land because Saul had broken the agreements that Joshua had made with the Gibeonites.

> *Now there was a famine in the days of David for three years, year after year; and David inquired of the Lord. And the Lord answered, "It is because of Saul and his bloodthirsty house because he killed the Gibeonites."*
>
> *2 Samuel 21:1*

---

[69]   Psalm 15:4

Covenants Have Power Over Many Generations

We have come to the heart of the matter. Every covenant has the power of law, meaning that each party can go to a judge when the agreements made in the covenant are not respected. The legal power of a covenant is greater when this covenant has been sealed with blood. This is also true when the covenant is made by people who are in a position of authority that is recognized by heaven. A covenant has greater legal power when the leaders of a city, a nation, or an organization make it.

Satan knows very well that a covenant is a binding force in the courts of heaven, especially when it is empowered with blood. This is why he seduces the leaders of a nation to seal a blood covenant with him. We see a very sad example in the history of Haiti.[70] The first leaders of this nation gained their freedom because they made a blood covenant, and in exchange, they dedicated the nation to satan.

The African slaves suffered under the dominion of the French. At the end of the eighteenth century, a group of slaves decided to rebel against them. The leaders of this revolt made a covenant, in 1791, with the spiritual powers of their ancestors. They sacrificed a gazelle, a pig, and a goat. These leaders drank the pig's blood and solemnly swore that they would rather die than live in slavery. Shortly after this, a rebellion broke out. In 1804, independence was declared. The first sovereign republic of Africans in the Western Hemisphere was born.

Haiti was the first nation in the world where slaves successfully gained their freedom. But an enormous price was paid to make this possible. Even today, more than two hundred years later, the Haitians experience the consequences of the covenant that their ancestors made with satan. Haiti is by far the poorest nation in the Western Hemisphere. It is part of the Island Hispaniola. The other part of this island is the Dominican Republic and the difference between these two nations couldn't be greater.

On satellite images, you can see the border between these two nations. On the Dominican side, there is reasonable prosperity. Life expectancy is high and there are several touristic retreats. The Haitian side of the

---

[70] From slave revolt to a blood pact with satan, E. McAlister, Wesleyan University 2012.

border is drastically different. The ground is barren and infertile. Life expectancy is much lower, and a large portion of the citizens live in abject poverty. There are 229 countries listed in a 2016 economic survey. The Dominican Republic is ranked 74. Haiti, on the other hand, is ranked 174. The Netherlands is ranked 28 for comparison.[71]

Every covenant has legal power.

Exactly 200 years later, in 1991, president Jean-Bertrand Aristide renewed the covenant by drinking pig's blood. In 2010, there was a terrible earthquake in Haiti. When evangelist Pat Robertson pointed to the differences between the consequences of the environmental disaster between Haiti and the Dominican Republic, he endured a torrent of criticism. When Robertson connected the results of this earthquake with the blood covenant that was made with satan in 1791 and was renewed in 1991, even the White House condemned his statement. It is my opinion that he spoke the truth. Later, more articles were written that supported Robertson in his opinion.

The Covenant Is A Form of Trading

The strength of a covenant is founded upon the equivalence of both parties and the promise to keep the terms of the contract. If a covenant is made, both parties trade something. Like we saw earlier, marriage is an example of a covenant between two people. Both parties are equal. Both parties agree to bring their part to the table. When a covenant is made, an exchange takes place. The marriage covenant is sealed with blood, assuming both partners are virgins when they enter this covenant.

The sacrifice of Jesus on the cross empowers the greatest covenant ever made in creation. It is a covenant between the Almighty God and humanity. We are equal covenant partners in the eyes of God. He made a covenant with us even when He knew that we were not capable to fulfill our part of the deal. This is why He Himself became a human being and fulfilled all the requirements of this covenant as the Son of Man. That is

---

[71] https://www.cia.gov/library/publications/the-world-factbook/rankorder/2001rank.html#dr

why we are entitled to the blessings of the covenant God made with mankind. The greatest trade mankind has ever known was made at the cross. Derek Prince has written a book about this great truth.[72]

You might know the popular worship song entitled, *Trading My Sorrows*.[73] The lyrics of this song show us the power of the cross. The sacrifice of Jesus has tremendous legal power in the courts of heaven. It is there that we can trade our sickness for healing, our poverty for riches, and our shame for honor.

> *And you, being dead in your trespasses and the uncircumcision of your flesh, He has made alive together with Him, having forgiven you all trespasses, having wiped out the handwriting of requirements that was against us, which was contrary to us. And He has taken it out of the way, having nailed it to the cross. Having disarmed principalities and powers, He made a public spectacle of them, triumphing over them in it.*
>
> *Colossians 2:13-15*

The handwriting mentioned in this passage is a legal document where all the evidence of our sins is recorded. Satan searches these dossiers in order to press charges against us. But when we confess our sins, all the evidence that testifies against us is nailed to the cross and destroyed. But as long as we keep silent, the evidence still exists.

When we humble ourselves before God, we are able to triumph over all our enemies and powers in darkness. It is the blood of Jesus that testifies on our behalf and makes it possible for us to claim the blessings recorded in Deuteronomy 28.

This mechanism of trading is an integral part of the court system in heaven. Every legal transaction made in heaven has something to do with trading. We may think that our salvation is for free, but that is not true. Someone had to pay a terrible price for the salvation of our souls. That is why we glorify Jesus Christ, the Son of the living God. He has, by His death, fulfilled all the requirements of the law of the covenant, so that we can obtain the legal right to become sons of God.[74]

---

[72] Bought with Blood: The Divine Exchange at the Cross DPM International, 2000.
[73] Written by Israel Houghton & New Breed, 2001.
[74] John 1:12

> We will only receive the benefits of the covenant when we are
> willing to trade something in return.

Without this exchange it is not possible to operate in the kingdom of heaven. The secrets of the kingdom are only available for the disciples of Jesus. But we only become disciples when we choose to leave everything behind to follow Jesus. That is the price to be paid; the trade being made. Some believe that everything in the kingdom should be for free, but this is a misconception and a trap, precisely for the reasons I mentioned here. We will only receive the benefits of the covenant when we are willing to trade something in return.

That is why I don't believe in free spiritual education and conferences. This is not because I believe the one teaching you should make a lot of money. Rather, it is important for those who are listening. When you really want to be an owner of the revelation, you should trade something in return. These are the principles that apply on the earth and in the kingdom of heaven. This is the essence of making a covenant; both parties bring something to the table. That is why Jesus told the Laodiceans that they should buy from Him. They were wretched, miserable, poor, blind, and naked because they were lukewarm and prideful.

> *I counsel you to buy from Me gold refined in the fire, that you may be rich; and white garments, that you may be clothed, that the shame of your nakedness may not be revealed; and anoint your eyes with eye salve, that you may see.*
>
> *Revelations 3:18*

It is God's desire that we are rich, clothed, and can see. But it is up to us to pay the price for this—to ask how we can buy from Him and how we can pay Him. It is not always with money that we bring our share into the covenant. It can be in our time, our abilities, and our care for others. This is the essence of making a covenant; both parties trade something that is dear to them.

The Consequences in The Court of Heaven

We have seen the consequences of making a covenant. A covenant is not without obligations; we are compelled to fulfill the requirements of the covenant. These obligations are passed on to future generations who will also be under these terms. This is why we have to deal with any covenants made by our ancestors.

At the moment any of our ancestors made a covenant with satan, we were bound to the consequences, even if the covenant was made under deceitful circumstances. If this covenant has had adverse consequences, we are, according to the laws of the heavenly dimensions, obliged to fulfill the terms of this covenant. Every covenant is a contract that has legal power---on earth *and* in the heavenly dimensions. Our adversary can accuse us before the Heavenly Judge when we do not keep the terms and agreements of the covenant.

This is precisely satan's objective—to make covenants with men, with terms that give him the right to control future generations. We can see this in Freemasonry. The person who makes the covenant benefits directly from it in his lifetime. A contract is signed where the person--in exchange for power, wealth, and protection--dedicates his future generations to satan. Satan now has the legal right to claim control over those lives in the courts of heaven. He is legally allowed to hinder those future generations from reaching their God-given destiny. These covenants are so sinister because they are made with the powers of darkness. It is possible that you did nothing wrong but are dealing with secret schemes made by your ancestors.

But on the other hand, these principles can also be applied to the covenants that are made by our ancestors with the Almighty God. We now receive the benefits from these ancient contracts. The point is that these benefits are also available for the future generations who come after us. The price to receive these blessings and benefits was paid by Christ on the cross. Notice that God says, in the ketubah He made with the people of Israel, that for the one who serves Him a thousand future generations after him will be blessed.[75]

---

[75] Exodus 20:6

George Otis Jr. has extensively written in his book, *The Twilight Laby-rinth,* how nations have made covenants with the powers and principalities in darkness.[76] In such a covenant, the nation might receive protection, such as from environmental disasters. The leader who makes the covenant always receives the benefits in his lifetime. We see this when dictators live like a king in luxury and have loaded secret bank accounts in Switzerland, but their country is literally surrendered to demons.

There is one condition—each covenant must be annually renewed. We see this with the covenants that God has made with His people. Every year the high priest would enter the Holy of Holies and renew the covenant that God made with Moses and was sealed with a blood sacrifice. Nowadays, we see this occur with our cultural festivals. While the people celebrate, these rituals are quietly carried out in the background, empowering the covenants with blood sacrifices.

For example, there is a well-known festival called the Hindu Dasain festival in Nepal, where hundreds of thousands of animals are slaughtered and their blood flows through the streets to dedicate their country to the idols. Another example is in South American countries during Carnival, where blood is sacrificed to renew the ancient covenants.[77]

Dissolving of Covenants

This raises a question. How can we dissolve the covenants that our ancestors made with satan? I am not only talking about our own lives, but also about cities, nations, and organizations. We'll discuss the details further in Part 2 of this book; here we will discuss the outlines.

It is important to understand that only someone who has legal authority can dissolve the covenant. The mandate he carries must be recognized in heaven. As a citizen, we are not authorized to dissolve a covenant with the powers of darkness that has been made by a mayor of a city or the president of a nation. The person who dissolves the covenant must have the proper mandate. I will discuss this in a later chapter.

---

[76] Published by Chosen books in 1997
[77] http://blogs.reuters.com/faithworld/2009/02/21/llama-sacrifices-in-a-bolivian-mine-at-carnival/

To dissolve a covenant, you first must waive all the benefits you received. This is an important prerequisite. You need to renounce every gain you had--everything that satan or other powers of darkness have exchanged with you or your ancestors. This might include protection, prosperity, position, wealth, or power.

This often happens when convicted criminals come to Jesus. The main reason for their criminal actions was often the financial gain. Their financial wealth enabled them to have an exorbitant lifestyle. Many times, the financial supply dries up at the moment they repent. They fall from great wealth into great poverty in a very short time. This is often the most difficult phase they encounter during their recovery. When they persevere, the power that the enemy has over them will eventually be broken.

Which Steps Do You Need to Take?

There are several steps you need to take in order to dissolve a covenant with satan. It begins with repentance, by or on behalf of the person who originally made the covenant. Next, you publicly renounce all the benefits gained from the covenant.

We call on the blood of the Lamb as a propitiation for all the demands that were made in the covenant made with satan. Jesus stands at our side and He is our Advocate, pleading for us.[78] The power of the blood is activated by the words of our confession of our sins.

Jesus then states that all the evidence that testifies against us is destroyed because they are nailed to the cross by our confession.[79] This also applies to all covenants that were made by our ancestors. Instead of the destruction of our lives and destiny, we receive in return the blood of Christ. Try to imagine what happens in the domain of the prince of darkness at the moment we confess our sins.

It is essential that we receive the divorce papers when the Judge of all has dissolved the covenant. Because a covenant has legal status, there must be an official document where its termination has been recorded. This document is also mentioned by Moses and is called the certificate of divorce, or divorce paper. It is important that the Judge signs these

---

[78]   1 John 2:1
[79]   Colossians 2:14

divorce papers. It is an official record in the courts of heaven stating that we are no longer obliged to keep the terms of the covenant. The moment we are accused, we only need to show these important documents to our accuser. This document revokes every legal right satan has to accuse us, to hinder us, to curse us, or to obstruct us---but only if we have confessed our sins in this matter and called upon the blood of Christ.

It is essential that we receive the divorce papers
when the Judge of all has dissolved the covenant.

As soon as the documents are signed, we make a new covenant, but this one is with our God and Father. We declare that we belong to Him and that we are entitled to receive the benefits of the greatest covenant ever made. This covenant is empowered by blood through the sacrifice of Jesus Christ on the cross.

Is the Sacrifice of The Cross Sufficient?

I understand when Christians ask, "Didn't Jesus conquer satan on the cross? Why do we have to do all these difficult things in the court of heaven?"

It is true that Jesus made a public spectacle of all demonic principalities. Jesus is sitting at the right hand of His Father. He entered the glory of His Father and is crowned with all power, glory, and beauty. This is all true. But still, Jesus is waiting on something more. He waits until all His enemies are made His footstool.

But this Man, after He had offered one sacrifice for sins forever, sat down at the right hand of God, from that time waiting till His enemies are made His footstool.

Hebrews 10:12-13

After Jesus ascended to heaven with the clouds of witnesses, He was brought before the Ancient of Days. There He was crowned and received all honor and glory. He obtained the right to sit at the right hand of His Father.

But, even then the battle on earth continues. We read this in the seventh chapter of Daniel. The saints of the Most High encounter a fierce battle; some do not survive. Still, the war goes on. There are still powers of darkness that have not bent their knees. Still the nations rage and rebel against the throne. The people plot a vain thing against the Lord and His Anointed. This speaks of Jesus sitting next to His Father after He died on the cross and ascended.

> *The kings of the earth set themselves, and the rulers take counsel to-gether, against the Lord and against His Anointed, saying, "Let us break Their bonds in pieces and cast away Their cords from us."*
>
> *Psalm 2:2-3*

In the last 40 days that Jesus walked the earth, He spoke quite intention-ally with His disciples. They didn't take a trip down memory lane. They didn't talk about all the miracles, signs, and wonders Jesus did. They didn't talk about the reaction of the Sanhedrin after He rose from the dead. No, Jesus talks with them about the kingdom of heaven. That was the only thing that mattered to Him.[80] During this time, they received the commandment to subdue all His enemies at the feet of Jesus, in the power of the sacrifice of the cross and His blood. *Go out into the entire world and proclaim the Gospel of the kingdom of heaven to all nations...*

Apparently, the commandment to bring His enemies down is so im-portant that it is recorded seven times in the Bible. This is the command-ment that Christ gave to His church that we have forgotten for centuries. It is our sworn duty to bring all His enemies as a footstool to His feet. The important question now is: "Where is this footstool located?" The book of Acts reveals this.

> *Heaven is My throne, and earth is My footstool. What house will you build for Me? says the Lord, or what is the place of My rest?*
>
> *Acts 7:48*

This passage reveals the relationship between the throne and the foot-stool of Jesus. We do not conquer the enemy by fighting on the battlefield. We conquer them first in the courts of heaven where justice is achieved and verdicts are rendered.

It is so important for us to understand that the kingdom of heaven is founded on righteousness and justice. Everything that happens in the kingdom has a legal status. Every calling, anointing, and sacrifice that has

---

[80]   Acts 1:3-9

been made has a legal basis. The church has the task to revoke every legal right the enemy has to dominion upon the earth. As long as there are human beings on the earth that make covenants with satan, he has control and dominion in the territory and sphere of influence of that person. The higher the position that person has on earth, the greater the control satan has in that domain.

The sacrifice of Jesus on the cross has the greatest legal power. Jesus testifies in heaven on our behalf, but a matter can only be established by the mouth of two or three witnesses.[81] This is why people living on the earth need to give their testimony in the courts of heaven. This is one of the reasons we were sent to the ends of the earth; to bring testimony from every region of the earth into heaven. It is important that our testimony is in agreement with the testimony of Jesus.

To be a witness means more than just telling the story of the death and resurrection of Jesus. The Bible uses the word "testify" as giving an official statement in a court of law. The Greek word for testimony is *martys*, where the word martyr comes from. A martyr is someone who is willing to speak the truth even if it will cost him his life. Jesus asks us to be witnesses on the earth so that heaven and earth offer one and the same testimony. We are to testify from the earth in the courts of heaven and agree with the testimony that Jesus is giving there.

> We conquer the enemy first in the courts of heaven,
> where justice is achieved and verdicts are rendered.

This is how the will of God can be done on earth. Now He can render a verdict that is united with His passion for us. That is why we, as the Body of Christ, should defeat the enemy in the courts of heaven first. Then we will see righteousness and justice done on the earth. Only when all the enemies are conquered and made into a footstool will Jesus triumphantly return as the King of Kings amidst all His saints that have overcome.

---

[81] Deuteronomy 19:15

Conclusion

Every covenant that is made on the earth has legal power in heaven. Be it between people, tribes, nations, or with the powers of darkness, every party is obliged to meet the terms of the covenant. Dissolving a covenant can only be done by someone that has the right mandate to do so. We have seen how later generations are bound by the terms of the covenant. Therefore, let us be diligent to do research on the obligations, oaths, and covenants that our ancestors left us as an inheritance—both good and evil.

Jesus is sitting on the throne at the right hand of His Father. He is waiting until all His enemies are made into a footstool. The earth is His footstool; it is up to us to conquer all the enemies of the cross. We don't do this by fighting against them on the earth. We do this from the courts of heaven by taking away every legal ground that gives satan the right to have dominion on the earth. This is how we are victorious over every enemy of Christ and make them a footstool for His feet. That is what Jesus is waiting for. This is what Hebrews 10:13 tries to tell us: Jesus is waiting from that time "till His enemies are made His footstool."

Only after we have dealt with the legal grounds in the courts of heaven can we be victorious on the earth. This is why the revelation of the courts of heaven is so important and why we are called to testify there. We need to raise our voice from the earth so that it is heard in heaven so that the testimonies in heaven and the testimonies from the earth will be one. That is the basis for the execution of the verdict over the enemies of God.

In the next chapter, we will see the mandate we have to operate in the courts of heaven. The premise we have is our destiny, as we have received from our Father.

7

What Is Our Mandate?

This question about our personal mandate is very important and we must answer it next. Operating in the courts of heaven will be extremely difficult if we don't know what our personal mandate is.

To answer this question, we first have to understand the meaning of a mandate. When you have received a mandate, you are authorized to act on someone's behalf, but the final responsibility remains with the person who has mandated you.

I will give an example of how a mandate can operate in normal life. Suppose you are the purchasing agent of a company. You are responsible to maintain the supplies that keep production going. Your employer has mandated you to contact suppliers in order to purchase and pay for the necessary items. You are not responsible for the balance on the account; your employer is. But there is a limit. If your order exceeds a preset limit you have to contact your employer. And of course, you can't buy personal stuff on your employer's account. You need a mandate in order to fulfill your job and your employer will keep you accountable for the transactions.

The Scroll and The Counsel of the Lord

Jesus came to the earth in order to fulfill the assignment that was written beforehand in the scroll of His life. Everything that happened in the life of Jesus was the result of a counsel of the Lord. We see that Peter and John knew about these decrees of the Holy One. When they return from their court session at the Sanhedrin, they testify:

> *For of a truth against your holy child Jesus, whom You have anointed, both Herod, and Pontius Pilate, with the Gentiles, and the people of Israel, were gathered together, for to do whatever Your hand and Your counsel determined before to be done.*
>
> *Acts 4:27-28 [A-KJV]*

Even Paul was aware that the plans of God for his life were determined before he was born. He was separated and equipped to fulfill the assignment God had prepared for him. We, too, are on the earth to do the good works God has ordained.[82] He equips us and gives us everything we need in order to be successful.

> *But when it pleased God, who separated me from my mother's womb and called me through His grace, to reveal His Son in me, that I might preach Him among the Gentiles.*
> *Galatians 1:15-16*

Everyone receives a scroll from heaven. These scrolls contain the assignment that God gives to each and every human being. When we are on the earth, it is our duty to fulfill this assignment. He has called us through His grace and equipped us to be successful. This is the essence of our destiny. We see in the life of Jesus that He was fully aware of His assignment.

> *Therefore, when He came into the world, He said: "Sacrifice and offering You did not desire, but a body You have prepared for Me. In burnt offerings and sacrifices for sin You had no pleasure. Then I said, 'Behold, I have come— In the volume of the book it is written of Me— To do Your will, O God.'"*
> *Hebrews 10:5-7*

We have fulfilled our destiny on the earth when we have successfully executed all assignments that we have received by the counsel of the Lord. We see this in the life of David. He died only after he had accomplished everything that was written about him in the counsel of the Lord.

> *For David, after he had in his own generation served the counsel of God, fell asleep, and was laid unto his fathers, and saw corruption.*
> *Acts 13:36 [ASV]*

Every decision that has been taken by the throne is called a counsel of the Lord. We also see this in the Dutch governmental system. Every law that is decreed by the government and every formal nomination must be signed by the king of the Netherlands. Only after the king has signed the document does it receive the force of law. The document in which the decision of the king is recorded is called a Royal Decree.

---

82 Ephesians 2:10

Imagine that someone is seriously ill and is likely to die before their time, at an age and in a manner that is not according to the plan and intention of God. According to this verse, we have received the mandate to pray for those who are sick or dying before it is their time because their task isn't finished. When we pray for them in the courts of heaven, it is essential that we do not plead according to the emotions we experience at that moment.

When we are in a courtroom, the judge doesn't rule according to the emotions in the case, but according to the lawfulness of the actions of both parties; according to the principles of righteousness and justice. Our defense in court is based on the realization of our destiny and on everything that is written in the counsel of the Lord. If someone hasn't fulfilled their God-given destiny as recorded in their scroll, we can plead before the Judge that the enemy cannot destroy their life. We see this in the life of Job. God doesn't allow satan to kill Job.

And the Lord said to Satan, "Behold, he is in your hand, but spare his life."

Job 2:6

Mandate is Connected to Our Destiny

The destiny that God has given you is a unique, personal assignment. There is no one on the earth that can fulfill your assignment in the manner by which you can do it. Therefore, it is useless to be jealous of the ministry of someone else.

But you can learn something when you are feeling jealous. You only become jealous of someone who has a similar destiny to yours. Every time you say to yourself: "I could do that better," or "Why aren't they asking me to do that?" you are provoked in your spirit. People that have similar destinies are spiritually connected in one way or the other.

But you have received your own assignment from God. Everything that happens in your life can and will be used by Him in order to help you to fulfill your assignment.[83] He has called you according to His purpose.

---

83 Romans 8:28

He has given you your talent, your abilities, the right personality, and the mandate to fulfill this assignment successfully.

The enemy knows this all too well. He will try by any means to hinder you in fulfilling your assignment because everyone who realizes their God-given destiny is a direct threat for the domain of satan. The adversary of God can't stand it when we are successful in the kingdom of heaven. He is furious when the children of God realize their potential on earth, even if it is only one person.

This was the case with Haman the Agagite, the enemy of the Jews, as we read in the book of Esther.[84] While everyone was kneeling before him as the king commanded them to, Haman was furious when one man refused to do so: Mordecai, the Jew.

This incited hatred in Haman, but this hatred became his downfall. God only needed one man, Mordecai, to bring down the archenemy of Israel. This is how he fulfilled his assignment within his God-given mandate. It was Mordecai who took over the position of Haman in the end. Where the enemy tried to destroy a nation, God intervened because there was one person still standing.

> Our mandate is connected to our destiny
> and the position we have obtained in heaven.

When we are standing in the mobile court, our mandate there is directly connected to our assignment as it is written in our scroll. When the enemy stands against us, our only plea in the court of heaven is the fulfillment of our destiny. We should not plead from our personal needs, our emotions, the distress we are experiencing, or for help with our problems. He delivers us from our enemies, not our problems.[85] In the mobile court, it all comes down to the fulfillment of our God-given destiny, as recorded and ratified by the counsel of the Lord. That is the basis for our court case and that is the legal ground for our mandate.

This is what Moses did when he pleaded for the salvation of his own nation before God. God was very angry at Israel because He was deeply

---

[84] Esther 3:1-5
[85] Psalm 7 and many more

hurt by their actions and sins. He wanted to destroy the nation and make a great nation out of Moses. But Moses argued strenuously with Him, reminding Him of His promises and of the destiny of the nation of Israel.

> *Then Moses pleaded with the Lord his God, and said: "Lord, why does Your wrath burn hot against Your people whom You have brought out of the land of Egypt with great power and with a mighty hand? Why should the Egyptians speak, and say, "He brought them out to harm them, to kill them in the mountains, and to consume them from the face of the earth'? Turn from Your fierce wrath and relent from this harm to Your people. Remember Abraham, Isaac, and Israel, Your servants, to whom You swore by Your own self, and said to them, 'I will multiply your descendants as the stars of heaven; and all this land that I have spoken of I give to your descendants, and they shall inherit it forever."' So the Lord relented from the harm which He said He would do to His people.*
>
> *Exodus 32:11-14*

Moses used a powerful weapon in this court session. He reminded God of the promises He made to the descendants of Abraham concerning their destiny. God pledged Himself under oath with the people of Israel. Every promise that God decrees from His throne is written down in a council decision, royal decree, or counsel of the Lord. The basis for the plea of Moses is found in these written heavenly scrolls.

The Extent of Our Mandate

The extent of our mandate in the courts of heaven is directly connected with the promises and the assignments recorded in heaven. Every person has the mandate to plead for the realization of their own destiny. God has granted us the right to silence every tongue that speaks against us in the courts of heaven.

> *"No weapon formed against you shall prosper, and every tongue which rises against you in judgment You shall condemn. This is the heritage of the servants of the Lord, and their righteousness is from Me," Says the Lord.*
>
> *Isaiah 54:17*

This verse clearly states that we have the mandate to testify in the courts of heaven. It is our heritage; in fact, it is our duty. When we do not fulfill our destiny, the kingdom of heaven will suffer. Every destiny that is destroyed is a victory for the enemy of God. It is vital that we know what our destiny is, and that we are aware of our responsibilities, on earth as in heaven.

The mandate that we have received from God is directly connected with the responsibility we carry. This responsibility is connected with our destiny, with the function we have, or in the office we carry. Everything is written down in our personal scroll, and it is important that we read this scroll and make it our own.

Sometimes we are not only responsible for the realization of our own destiny but also for the destinies of others. It can be that God has given us a position in which we carry the responsibility to bring people who are entrusted to our care before the Lord. When we stand before the face of God, we plead and ask forgiveness on their behalf. In this manner, we grant God the right to forgive them and to bless them.

> The mandate we receive from God is directly
> connected with the responsibility we carry.

Sometimes, other people can ask us to act on their behalf. For example, this happens in an earthly court where we are represented by a lawyer. We give the lawyer a mandate to defend our case before the judge. In Scripture, we see that the leaders of the cities in Israel asked the prophets to pray for their city. A well-known example is when leaders of Jericho asked Elisha to pray for the barrenness in the land.[86]

The Mandate to Plead

A lawyer friend of mine told me the story of a court case where he legally represented someone in a legal matter. On behalf of his client, he submitted several claims as the plaintiff, in order to prevent the eviction from his residence. The homeowner was allowed to defend his case before the judge, but he himself was not present during the session. Instead, he sent a bailiff to represent him.

---

[86] 2 Kings 2:19-22

When the judge allowed the defendant to speak, he asked the homeowner's representative, who he was, and who he was representing. The bailiff told the judge that he represented the homeowner and began to address the judge on the matter.

But the judge stopped him and would not allow him to speak in the court session. Speaking was a right that was only available for the homeowner or his lawyer. Because the plaintiff was neither, he wasn't allowed to speak on behalf of the homeowner. He didn't have the legal mandate to represent the homeowner.

The bailiff objected, saying he had done this in several other cases throughout the country. But the judge held firm, stating that he was presiding over this court and would strictly follow the law. The judge granted all claims to my friend's client. In this case, we see that it is very important to appear in court with the right mandate to plead.

Satan is our adversary in the courts of heaven, and he will use every legal trick in the book in order to prevent us to defend our case. He knows that if we plead in the right manner, his case is already lost. If we are going to plead on behalf of someone else, we need to carry the proper mandate.

Not only do people have a destiny from heaven, but also cities, districts, states, and nations. Even corporations and organizations can be recognized in heaven and have a scroll there with their destiny written on it. In this scroll, it is also written who is responsible for the realization of this destiny. That can be a person, a board of directors, or a government official. Only these people are allowed, in principle, to represent or plead for their organization or nation in the courts of heaven. However, it is possible that other people can receive the mandate to speak on their behalf in court.

When someone pleads in the courts of heaven for a nation, a city, or an organization, the enemy pays very close attention to whether or not you have the proper mandate. If you don't have the proper mandate, the enemy can ask the judge to declare your plea inadmissible in court. This is what happens to a lot of intercessors. Despite the enormous passion they have when they pray, their pleas are not allowed in court because they do not have the right mandate. The judge can't consider their testimony or pleas when he rules a case.

Therefore, it is so important to know if you have the proper mandate when you plead for your nation or city because your mandate is always connected with the God-given responsibility and the outcome.

The Mandate to Judge

Do we have the mandate to judge? Are we authorized to render a verdict? Many Christians believe that only God has the authority to judge. They refer to the Sermon on the Mount in Matthew, where Jesus says that we should not judge. Of course, this is true, but Jesus isn't finished speaking. There is a reason we should not judge.

Judge not, that you be not judged. For with what judgment you judge, you will be judged; and with the measure you use, it will be measured back to you. And why do you look at the speck in your brother's eye, but do not consider the plank in your own eye?

Matthew 7:1-3

We should not judge if we have a plank in our own eye. Only after we have taken the plank out of our own eye are we able to help our brother.

Again, I want to emphasize what happens with our emotions when we hear the word *judgment*. We often have a negative response, which is rooted in the fear we have for the final judgment. But Jesus is talking about making a decision about good and evil, not about the final judgment.

Do not judge according to appearance, but judge with righteous judgment.

John 7:24

If it is true that a Christian cannot judge, then no Christian could ever be an earthly judge. I think we all know that we need judges to uphold law and order in society. Without a proper judicial system, everyone would merely do what is good in their own sight. Chaos and anarchy would be free to reign. Every society and community need an administration of justice in order to resolve conflicts. Jesus is warning us not to judge when our own judgment is clouded. As long as there is a plank in our eyes, we should restrain ourselves from judging. By the measure we use to judge, we shall be judged.

The Greek word for judging is *krino*. This verb appears 115 times in the New Testament. Some of these passages talk about the final judgment and others mention the judgment that is placed in the hands of Jesus. But there are also passages where Paul explains that the saints of God have the mandate to judge.

> *Dare any of you, having a matter against another, go to law before the unrighteous, and not before the saints? Do you not know that the saints will judge the world? And if the world will be judged by you, are you unworthy to judge the smallest matters? Do you not know that we shall judge angels? How much more, things that pertain to this life?*
>
> *1 Corinthians 6:1-3*

The situation in Corinth was starting to get out of hand. The tension between the members of this church was increasing. People were taking sides and the unity of the body of Christ was being threatened. Paul wrote about this in his first letter. Members of the first church had begun to pursue justice in secular courts by those who are not qualified or mandated to judge about spiritual matters.

Paul told them they were wrong, indirectly referring to the local court: the Beth Din of the synagogue (as I mentioned previously). According to Jewish regulations, the members of the Beth Din were mandated to render a verdict over internal conflicts between the members of the synagogue. It was erroneous for the members of the church in Corinth to seek justice there. Paul even reminded them that the saints of the Most High not only judge the world, but also the angels.

We are priests and kings before God
because we are seated with Him.

If saints are mandated to judge angels, then they surely must be mandated to judge things that pertain to this normal life. We are appointed to judge with Christ, not only in the future but also today.

I will try to explain this. Christ is seated in the heavenlies far above every principality, power, might, and dominion. He rules over them. He is the Head over all things.

Through God's mercy, we too are raised from the dead and made alive. We are seated with Christ in the heavenlies on the throne, next to the Father. Paul explains this in Ephesians 1:20-2:8

A throne is a place to render a verdict of judgment, as it is intimately connected to the office and position of a king. We are priests and kings before God *because* we are seated with Him. This is the position from which we judge the world and the angels. It is a privilege and mandate that is given to us.

But most of us miss this opportunity to rule because we are uncertain if we are allowed or mandated to do this. We scarcely dare to bring our problems before the face of our God, and we are only partially convinced that He hears us. We don't take up the responsibility to act in judgment of the enemy. We wait for our Daddy in heaven to solve all of our problems. But that is not a mature attitude.

When we first converted to Christianity, we were like little children, solely dependent on others. We needed to be fed, nurtured, and clothed. Others were held accountable for our welfare and we often called for help. But God wants us to become mature sons. He has called to us be responsible for what is happening on the earth. He has given us the assignment to establish His kingdom here. He has called us to become kings and priests in heaven. It is the duty of kings to judge and render a verdict from their throne; to scatters all evil with His eyes.

A king who sits on the throne of judgment scatters all evil with his eyes.

Proverbs 20:8

When there is no king in the land, chaos and anarchy break loose. Each one does as seems best in their own eyes. We see this principle at work in the book of Judge—a portion of the Bible that is completely dedicated to the function and position of judges in the nation of Israel. We read story after story of judges that arise when the nation is in distress. They bring justice in the nation and render verdicts. Each of these twelve judges brings the nation back to God. But alas, when each judge died, the nation again turns away from the Lord.

In those days there was no king in Israel; everyone did what was right in his own eyes.

Judges 17:6 and 21:25

Everybody understands that this is not a healthy condition for any nation. A nation without judges will end in chaos. Some believe that rules and regulations only limit their freedom, but nothing could be further from the truth. The rule of law secures our freedom; it is important to take our position in the heavenly courts, in order to defend our nation.

This means we need to grow up and accept the responsibilities of becoming a son. Often this brings us to a place of inner conflict. On one hand, we want to receive the power and glory that is connected to mature sonship, but on the other hand, we don't want to pay the price for it. When we make ourselves available to carry this responsibility, we receive the mandate to plead in the courts of heaven and to render verdicts.

> It is our assignment to train our senses
> to be able to discern both good and evil.

I fear that most of us are too dependent on milk and are incapable of digesting solid food. We prefer to be princes who can do mostly as we please and celebrate life to the fullest, rather than rising to become kings. We haven't learned yet to receive oracles from God and to apply them in our lives. After all, milk is the digested food of another living being. We are inexperienced in the word of righteousness and we haven't developed our senses to discern.

> *For though by this time you ought to be teachers, you need someone to teach you again the first principles of the oracles of God; and you have come to need milk and not solid food. For everyone who partakes only of milk is unskilled in the word of righteousness, for he is a babe.*
>
> *But solid food belongs to those who are of full age, that is, those who by reason of use have their senses exercised to discern both good and evil.*
>
> *Hebrews 5:12-14*

It is our assignment to train our senses to be able to discern both good and evil. This is the root meaning of the Greek word *krino*. When we render a verdict, we discern between good and evil. We should be the ones that let our voices be heard on the earth: "*This is injustice. We won't allow it."* Let us put aside trepidation and insecurity and take our positions as sons of God.

Now is the time to put this into practice and learn how to render a righteous verdict. We do this not with the intention to punish people or to prove ourselves right, but to be full of compassion, mercy, truth, and love. We judge in the same manner as we want to be judged by the Lord. Therefore, Jesus can plead for us because He was tested in the same way as we are. He knows how difficult it can be to walk on the earth in righteousness while experiencing temptation and desires. Jesus has the mandate to plead for us because He has overcome all temptations. This is His assignment as Priest in the house of His God.

> *Therefore, He is also able to save to the uttermost those who come to God through Him, since He always lives to make intercession for them.*
>
> *Hebrews 7:25*

The Mandate to Execute the Verdict

I have spoken extensively about the mandate to plead and to judge. But we have also received another mandate. This second mandate goes beyond the permission to judge. It gives us the authority to execute a verdict.

As I have said before, our mandate is directly connected with our destiny and position. We receive the mandate to execute the verdict when we have come to the maturity of sonship; when we become willing and able to carry responsibilities in the kingdom of heaven.

We find the basis for this mandate in the book of Psalms. We read that we execute written judgment and the manner by which we do it.

> *Let the saints be joyful in glory; let them sing aloud on their beds. Let the high praises of God be in their mouth, and a two-edged sword in their hand, to execute vengeance on the nations, and punishments on the peoples; to bind their kings with chains, and their nobles with fetters of iron; to execute on them the written judgment— this honor have all His saints. Praise the Lord!*
>
> *Psalm 149:5-9*

This Psalm is a triumphant song for the saints of the Lord. We receive the authority from God to execute written judgment on our enemies. We have the two-edged sword in our hand and the praises to our God on our lips. It is the Father's desire that we conquer our enemies because they are also His enemies. We execute the verdicts on the enemies of God on the earth.

For the last twenty years, I have been closely involved with deliverance ministry in our church. When we started this ministry in 1996, we had many among us who had encountered great traumas in their lives, such as severe forms of ritual abuse. This resulted in torment by demons and powers of darkness. What they experienced was very intense and they tried to find help for years. But nothing seemed to work or to help them.

> First and foremost, we are called to bless
> and love the people that stand against us.

One day, our church met someone who taught us a new way to pray for deliverance. This teaching was found to be a decisive key for the deliverance and redemption of our tormented church members. The essence of this key was that we don't fight the demon; rather, we open a case in the courts of heaven. We summoned the demons to come there and we held them accountable for all the misery they had caused their victims. You really can't imagine what it meant for these victims of ritual abuse when they literally saw that the demons had to answer to the Judge for what they had done. These heroes of God could see with their own eyes how the verdict of the Almighty Judge was executed upon the demons.

The results of these sessions were and still are amazing. We have seen the greatness of the sacrifice of Jesus with our own eyes. One of the key moments in each session was the execution of the verdict that the Eternal Judge had rendered over the demons. According to Psalms 149, we have received the authority to execute the final judgment on these powers in darkness. They are sometimes carried away in chains, other times they are cast into the abyss, or burned by the fire of the throne. One way or another, these verdicts are the end of an era of tyranny. For each of the heroes of our King, a new day had begun.

The mandate to execute the written judgments gives us the authority to sentence the punishment over the enemies of the Lord. Do you realize that the kings that are mentioned in Psalms 149 are not people, but are principalities and powers in darkness? Our battle is not against flesh and blood, but against the principalities and powers.[87] It is so important that we understand this. The enemies of the Lord are these principalities and powers in darkness, not the people that stand against us.

First and foremost, we are called to bless and love the people that stand against us. The Lord desires restoration with all His children. It is our task to support this desire of our Father by loving our counterparts and to pray for them. Just like Jesus, who died for us while we were enemies of the Father,[88] we can also give our lives for the restoration of our enemies. The essence of this book is that we learn how to intercede in the mobile court in such a way that the Judge will justify us. We don't enter the courts of heaven to drag His children before the Judge in order to get *them* convicted. After all, all souls belong to Him.[89]

Conclusion

We have received the mandate to enter the mobile courts of heaven. This is the place where we can plead, intercede, and judge. We have the privilege to execute on the earth the written judgment on His enemies. The extent of our mandate is directly connected with our destiny and the council decision of the Lord over our lives.

When we, as mature sons and daughters of the living God, take our assignment to act as kings on the earth seriously, there is hope for this creation. The whole creation awaits the revealing of the sons and daughters of God because it suffers the consequences of the unrighteousness of mankind.[90] I pray that we take our position in the courts of heaven so that we may lead this groaning creation into freedom.

In the next chapter, I will describe what we can do in the mobile court for the people that have wronged us.

---

[87] Ephesians 6:12
[88] Romans 5:8-10
[89] Ezekiel 18:4
[90] Romans 8:19, 22

8

Love Your Enemies

I have heard people aggressively declare their intention to sue their colleagues at work in the courts of heaven. They presume that they will come away as the victor and that their opponents will get what they deserve.

But this is in stark contrast with the nature and character of our God. The court of heaven is not the place to take someone for a ride. After all, the Almighty God is completely impartial. When we don't understand this, we have no clue who the righteous Judge really is. Scripture gives us many warnings to judge righteously in Israel. God hates false witnesses---judges who favor the rich and declare the guilty as not guilty.

When we present our case to the Heavenly Judge, He will not rule in our favor simply because we are His children. We can't go to the courts of heaven in order to solve all our problems. That is not the case in an earthly court, and it certainly is not the case in the heavenly one. The court of heaven is not a quick fix for our problems. If we are being truly honest, we can confess that when we face a conflict, we almost always view it through our paradigms and the lens of our emotions. This is almost inevitable because our emotions are deeply stirred when we are treated unjustly. Everything in us screams for revenge.

The court of heaven is not a quick fix for our problems.

When court is in session, several parties can speak and plead their case. There is the plaintiff, the defendant (and in criminal cases the district attorney and the defense counsel), witnesses, and expert witnesses. And there is a judge, whose duty is to give every party sufficient opportunity to state their case. The judge is also tasked with keeping order in the courtroom.

The court system does not make a ruling based on emotions. For instance, in the Netherlands, a civil judge can only render a verdict based on the facts. These facts need to be presented by the parties that stand before him. The judge himself is not allowed to present facts that could influence the outcome. Even if the judge is aware of certain facts that are not presented before him in the court, he is not allowed to consider these facts in his verdict.[91] Only after all parties have had the opportunity to present their case will he render a verdict.

Both parties have the right to appeal to the verdict of the judge. However, emotions are not sufficient grounds for the appeal. During the appeal, the case is judged on the compliance of the law, not on our emotional response to the verdict. We sometimes have great difficulty with a ruling that is in conflict with our sense of righteousness. But a judge is obliged to rule based on the law, not on his personal feelings about the case that is presented. What the judge thinks in private is not relevant.

These principles aren't much different in the courts of heaven. The Heavenly Judge will only render a verdict based on the facts and evidence that are presented during the case. If these are not presented in the right manner, the Heavenly Judge can't use them in His ruling, even if He, in His great love for us, would prefer to do it differently. This is the reason God became upset when there was no one to stand in the gap for the nation of Israel.

So I sought for a man among them who would make a wall, and stand in the gap before Me on behalf of the land, that I should not destroy it; but I found no one.

Ezekiel 22:30

The key to this verse is the passage: "stand before me." This shows us that we do not stand in the gap on the earth, but in the heavens---or better said, in the spiritual dimension. When we keep silent and refuse to stand in the gap, the only voice that is heard in the court of heaven is the voice of the accuser, satan. As John wrote, he accuses us day and night before our God.[92] Now is the time to let our voice be heard in the courts of heaven. It is our task to raise up a wall so that satan is no longer able to attack our nation or our loved ones.

---

[91] https://nl.wikipedia.org/wiki/Vonnis
[92] Revelations 12:10

Do Not Avenge Yourself

When we appear before an earthly court, we are represented by a lawyer who is well acquainted with the laws and protocol of the court. But we also need someone who can present the facts of our case without becoming emotional. When people become too emotional, the judge can adjourn the session or remove those who are disturbing order.

In most countries, it is forbidden to take the law into our own hands. We are not authorized to render a verdict against the one who has caused us hurt. When someone acts unjustly against us, we are obligated to present our case to a formal judge. He will render a verdict and will determine the sentence. He does this within the framework of the law and he uses the provisions the law provides.

Paul gives us the same advice. Don't be a judge, jury and, executioner, but give it all to God.

Repay no one evil for evil. Have regard for good things in the sight of all men. If it is possible, as much as depends on you, live peaceably with all men. Beloved, do not avenge yourselves, but rather give place to wrath; for it is written, "Vengeance is Mine, I will repay," says the Lord. Therefore "If your enemy is hungry, feed him; If he is thirsty, give him a drink; For in so doing you will heap coals of fire on his head."

Romans 12:17-20

Do you understand that forgiveness is a legal action? When you forgive someone, a record is made in heaven. In the legal file of your opponent, it is noted that you have given the right for retaliation into the hands of the Heavenly Judge. God is much better equipped to render a righteous verdict than we are. Check for yourself. When it is the other way around and you are being accused, aren't you pleading with God for mercy? We are very much capable to explain exactly why we did or didn't do a thing.

We argue before the Judge that it was never our intention to hurt the other person, or we explain to Him that the problem really lies with the other party. All of these arguments come from a single-minded perspective and from our soulish desire to be right. But if someone seems to be contentious, we should have no such custom.[93] The most important thing

---

[93] 1 Corinthians 11:16

is that the will of God is being fulfilled on the earth, just as it is done in heaven; an independent Judge that rules above all parties.

Fiery Coals

Scripture says: "If your enemy is hungry, feed him; If he is thirsty, give him a drink. Then you will heap coals of fire on his head." The Bible also tells us to love our enemies. These verses seem to be in contradiction. How can I love my enemy, all the while heaping fiery coals on his head?

A deep desire for retaliation remains within us. Sure, we will give food and drink to our enemies, but we do it with for a reason: let their heads be on fire. That will teach them a lesson.

Forgiveness is to relinquish the right for retaliation.

When we are thinking like this (and who doesn't?), we are still interpreting Scripture like a Greek and not like a Jew. Jews see the function of something, while the Greek is strictly looking at the form by which it is presented. We picture fiery coals that burn the head of our enemy. But in the Jewish perspective, the head stands for the government over something. When something is the head, it is leading the body. It governs and has authority over it. Remember what Paul wrote? He said that Christ is Head of the Ecclesia.

And He is the head of the body, the church, who is the beginning, the firstborn from the dead, that in all things He may have the preeminence.

Colossians 1:18

One of the Jewish principles of exegeses is called "the law of first mention," which means that you take a look at the first instance something is mentioned in Scripture. The context of this first mention sets the precedent for the other times we read about it. Now back to the fiery coals.

We first see this concept in Leviticus 16:12. We read about a censer full of burning coals which is brought as a sweet, fine-beaten incense beyond the veil by the High Priest.

With this context in mind, what does Scripture tells us we are doing when we love our enemy and give him food and a drink? By showing him love, we bring this person beyond the veil into the presence of our Lord. The fire of the altar will then burn the demonic power that is ruling over your enemy. Your enemies will be delivered from evil and oppression that they have experienced in *their* lives, in order to make them able to repent.

We don't go to the heavenly court to prove *our* point. When you enter with this attitude, it can end badly for you. It is Jesus Himself that warns us about this kind of thinking. In almost every conflict, there are two or more parties involved and responsible for the situation. An old saying proclaims: "It takes two to tango." When we justify ourselves entirely and blame our opponent for everything that happened, our adversary will deliver us to the Judge and prove us wrong.

Agree with your adversary quickly, while you are on the way with him, lest your adversary deliver you to the judge, the judge hand you over to the officer, and you be thrown into prison. Assuredly, I say to you, you will by no means get out of there till you have paid the last penny.

Matthew 5:25-26

No one, save the Lord, is without sin. In every conflict, we have played our role. It is better for you to acknowledge this before you appear in court. Our Heavenly Judge discerns every thought and intent of our heart.[94] Every word we have ever spoken and every thought we have ever had can be presented during the court session as evidence. Don't assume that your thoughts are hidden.

As for you, my son Solomon, know the God of your father, and serve Him with a loyal heart and with a willing mind; for the Lord searches all hearts and understands all the intent of the thoughts.

1 Chronicles 28:9

Do not curse the king, even in your thought; Do not curse the rich, even in your bedroom; For a bird of the air may carry your voice, and a bird in flight may tell the matter.

Ecclesiastes 10:20

---

94 Hebrews 4:12

Bless and Do Not Curse

When you make your plea in the courts of heaven, be merciful to those who have done you wrong. It can be very difficult to forgive someone who has done great injustice. We may need time to process this because our whole being screams for revenge. We must realize that the courts of heaven are there to judge the powers in darkness. They are not the place for our personal retaliation against people.

The most important choice that we can make is to allow Jesus to heal our heart. When His love has healed us, we can see the situation the way He does. It is easy to tell someone that he needs to forgive his enemies, especially if you haven't experienced trauma of your own. We need to ask God to retaliate for us. Perhaps this was the reason why David cried out for God to vindicate him.

We don't go to the heavenly court to prove *our* point.

To forgive people that have hurt us begins with a choice in the heart. Are we willing to let go of the pain and ask Jesus to help us with that? When we forgive someone, we don't pretend nothing has happened, or that God hasn't seen it. But when we forgive, we give God the opportunity to render a just verdict. Forgiveness, after all, is a legal act. When we forgive, we relinquish the right for retaliation to the righteous Judge. He can judge those who are ultimately responsible in a righteous and just manner.

How do I know if I have forgiven someone? The answer to this question is not as difficult as you might think. The degree by which we can publicly honor someone for who he really is, is the degree by which we have forgiven him. It is the degree by which we sincerely want him to be successful in realizing the assignment he has received from God. It is the degree by which we are willing to suffer for him to be successful in his walk with God. That is the trademark of forgiveness and we can only express it by letting the divine, agape of God flow through us.

If there is one word by which we can describe God, it is love. It is by His love that He sent His Son into the cosmos. It is this love that hopes everything, believes everything, and does anything it takes to restore relationship. It is this love that covers many sins. It is this love that saved our soul.

But God demonstrates His own love toward us, in that while we were still sinners, Christ died for us. For if when we were enemies we were reconciled to God through the death of His Son, much more, having been reconciled, we shall be saved by His life.

Romans 5:8,10

We are the ones that change when we forgive someone. We are set free from the pain, the bitterness, and the consequences of the injustice. The forgiveness that we proclaim sets *us* free.

But what about the verse in Scripture that tells us that if we forgive, God will forgive them too? What about retaliation for the injustice that has been done to us? When we read the context of this verse where Jesus talks about binding and loosing, we see that Jesus has given His disciples the authority to govern.[95]

If you forgive the sins of any, they are forgiven them; if you retain the sins of any, they are retained."

John 20:23

Jesus says to His disciples that when they judge and don't forgive someone, God as Judge won't forgive that person either.

A sad example is the story of Ananias and Sapphira.[96] They lie to the apostles, the church, and to the Holy Spirit about their financial gift, and the consequences are severe. Peter judges them both and they both die.

Don't think for a moment that God is pleased by the death of any human being, not even your enemies.[97] Do you know why David was a man after God's heart? He reacted the same way as God when he heard the news about the death of his enemy, Saul. When a young warrior tells David that Saul and his son Jonathan have been killed, he expects that David would be pleased to hear that. So, he starts bragging about the way they both died. He even pretends to have dealt the final blow of death. The way David and his men reacted was totally different than the warrior expected.

---

[95] Matthew 16:19
[96] Acts 5:1-11
[97] Ezekiel 18:23,32; Ezekiel 33:11

Therefore David took hold of his own clothes and tore them, and so did all the men who were with him. And they mourned and wept and fasted until evening for Saul and for Jonathan his son, for the people of the Lord and for the house of Israel because they had fallen by the sword.

2 Samuel 1:11-12

This David, the man who was driven from the king's court, hunted down for years, and sorely hated by Saul and his army, was genuinely grieved. David had been innocent and forced to flee for his life, but he tore his garments when he heard the news about the death of his enemy. He had already demonstrated that he wouldn't harm the Lord's anointed. When his men urged him to kill Saul because God placed Saul into David's hands, he chose not to. David didn't only respect the office of the king, he sincerely loved Saul and Jonathan.

The story doesn't end well for this young Amalekite. He was killed according to his own words: *I have killed the Lord's anointed.*

Let this be a lesson for all of us. God takes no pleasure in the death of a dying person, not even an ungodly one.[98] He calls every living being on the face of the earth to repentance. He loves them all. Let us follow His example, just like David did. God will always stand above the parties. The moment you are in conflict with another human being, you must realize that God loves this person as much as he loves you. He judges without respect of persons.

What About Companies in The Heavenly Courts?

When we appear in the courts of heaven to plead our case, we deal with individuals, though our real enemies are the devil and his powers in darkness. Satan is our adversary; the enemy who seeks to destroy us.

But we can also experience injustice from companies and organizations. Although the powers in darkness have great influence on companies and organizations, it is the people that function within these organizations that do us harm. When we appear in court concerning this injustice, we encounter the organization and companies, not the individuals

---

[98] Ezekiel 18:23

within it. They are our opponents, not our adversaries, and there is a difference.

Most companies and organizations have a mission statement, a destiny document if you will, to explain why they are on the earth. When this destiny is in line with the will of the Almighty One, the kingdom of God will be established through these companies and organizations. Heaven will support these organizations, and I personally believe there is a scroll in heaven for them. We should try to look at our opponent from a heavenly perspective.

Don't think for a moment that God is pleased by the death of any human being, not even your enemies.

For example, let's say you are in conflict with a company about the delivery of certain goods. The price and delivery date were agreed upon, but sometime later you get a phone call from the company. They now insist that you must pay a higher price because the product will be delivered by an alternate manufacturer. They explain why the price has gone up, but you want them to honor your order at the original price.

While you are preparing your court case, the Holy Spirit shows you why the company wants to change conditions. It appears that the company will receive a greater profit when they do business with the other manufacturer. This is the real reason why they are trying to wiggle into a different bargain.

So, what can you do? Of course, you can bring this company to the court of heaven and demand restitution. But the root of the problem is that the owner is unfairly seeking a greater profit. This is the influence of the mammon. The better approach is to bless the company so that it will be delivered from the influence of mammon, without loss of revenue. You don't curse the company because they succumbed to mammon. This is the proper attitude in the courts of heaven. You bless others who, just like you, have received an assignment from the Lord. It is your desire that they are just as successful as you want to be.

Although demons will have a negative influence on the people that work in the company, it is not the main issue. The heart of the matter is that you bless your opponent, even if they have wronged you. Forgiveness is a very powerful weapon in the court of heaven because it enables the Judge to give *you* justice. He will deal with every enemy that oppresses you and will reimburse you for everything that happened to you.

> *So I will restore to you the years that the swarming locust has eaten, the crawling locust, the consuming locust, and the chewing locust, My great army which I sent among you.*
>
> *Joel 2:25*

It is the assignment of the church to pray for companies, organizations, and people to set them free from demonic oppression. The principles that we discuss in this book aren't just applicable to our personal situations. They can be applied in other situations also. We can go to court for companies, cities, and nations. But that is beyond the scope of this book.

Speak A Blessing When You Plead

When we are able to bless our opponent, our Heavenly Father can deal with the real enemy: our adversary. After all, it is His desire that every person will have eternal life. Therefore, seek the best blessing for your opponent in the court of heaven. Bless people and organizations with the best that God can give them. Seek peace and live peaceably with all men.[99] Each person carries their own responsibility for the things they do. But we don't deny that demons can have a great influence on our behavior.

> *But I say to you, love your enemies, bless those who curse you, do good to those who hate you, and pray for those who spitefully use you and persecute you.*
>
> *Matthew 5:44*

When you are in court you do not speak to your opponent. You only address the Heavenly Judge. Of course, you are entitled to ask that your opponent honors the commitments that were made. But you do this with a different attitude. When you start praying for others and stand in the gap for them, you will sometimes be surprised by God. Your opponent might even change their opinion or approach.

This should be our attitude when we appear in the courts of heaven to appeal to the law. When we enter to destroy our opponent, who is

---

[99]   Romans 12:18

created in the image of God, we become blinded to what manner of spirit we are acting out of.[100] Proverbs warns us not to rejoice in the fall of our enemy.

> *Do not rejoice when your enemy falls, and do not let your heart be glad when he stumbles; lest the Lord see it, and it displease Him, and He turn away His wrath from him.*
>
> Proverbs 24:17-18

Paul gives us a similar warning. He says that we are not fighting against flesh and blood, but against the powers and principalities in high places. For this reason, it is important to prepare our court case. It is important that our pleas are not based on our emotions, but on the heart of God. Because the Heavenly Judge is also our Father and Friend, He will help us in this process. He may even ask you to stand in the gap for your opponent before you present your case against them.

When you are in court, you do not speak to
your opponent. You only address the Heavenly Judge.

When you start praying for your opponents and desire the best for them, it is amazing what happens to you after a few weeks. The Love of God starts to flow through you, and you will enter the courts of heaven with a different attitude. The victory of your court case becomes less important to you; you become eager to see that destinies become realized.[101] The kingdom of heaven suffers violence and the violent take it by force. This happens when we all start to fulfill our destinies.[102]

A Moment of Reflection

At the end of this chapter, I have an assignment for you. Please take a moment to reflect on times in which you reacted out of frustration or anger, speaking negatively about others. When you speak with a negative attitude, this is a form of cursing someone. Jesus is very clear about this.

---

[100] Luke 9:54-56
[101] 1 Corinthians 11:16
[102] Matthew 11:12

In the sermon on the mount, He advises how His followers should live their lives.

> *But I say to you that whoever is angry with his brother without a cause shall be in danger of the judgment. And whoever says to his brother, "Raca!" shall be in danger of the council. But whoever says, 'You fool!' shall be in danger of hell fire.*
>
> *Matthew 5:22*

The Greek word *Raca* means "empty-headed man." This is far from a swear word by our modern standards. We can easily find intense threads of similar insults on social media. But Jesus tells us here that when you are angry at your brother without cause, you will be charged guilty in the courts of heaven. Who hasn't occasionally had these thoughts? However, when you call him empty-headed, you will be judged by the high council. That is a strong statement.

Bless the people that you have cursed.
Give them the best that God has to offer them.

I want to ask you to consider the times that you've had negative thoughts and times you have spoken them aloud. Your words are going to be used by satan, not only to accuse your opponent, but also against *you*. He invokes this verse in Matthew 5:22. Ask the Holy Spirit if He wants to shine His Light in the depths of your heart. Repent from all the words that you have spoken out of anger. Recall them before the Lord your God and confess your sin. Bless the people you have cursed. Give them the best that God has to offer them. Then you have the right mindset by which to ask God for justice.

Conclusion

Let us go to the courts of heaven so we can see God's righteousness and justice being fulfilled on the earth. Let us go there in order to shape the will of God on earth. The courts of heaven aren't the place to destroy our enemies. They are meant to judge the real enemies of the kingdom—the devil and his demons. It is the place to make a public spectacle of them, triumphing over them. Let the verdict of the Heavenly Judge be on their heads!

Thus says the Lord of Hosts: "The children of Israel were oppressed, along with the children of Judah; all who took them captive have held them fast; they have refused to let them go. Their Redeemer is strong; the Lord of Hosts is His name. He will thoroughly plead their case, that He may give rest to the land, and disquiet the inhabitants of Babylon.

Jeremiah 50:33-34

God has given us great promises. He will avenge us and destroy our enemies. Every power that has tormented us will be destroyed by His fire. Then, like Jeremiah, we see that God will plead our case.

Therefore thus says the Lord: "Behold, I will plead your case and take vengeance for you."

Jeremiah 51:36a

We are so privileged because our God, our Redeemer, and our Father is also our Judge. He is for us and it is His desire to give us justice. He will give us freely all things.

What then shall we say to these things? If God is for us, who can be against us? He who did not spare His own Son, but delivered Him up for us all, how shall He not with Him also freely give us all things? Who shall bring a charge against God's elect? It is God who justifies.

Romans 8:31-33

In the next chapter, I will talk about the importance of the prophetic gifts in order to perceive what is going on in the courts of heaven.

9

Seeing In the Spiritual Dimension

How can I perceive what is going on in the courts of heaven? How do I enter these courts? How do I know how the Judge has ruled my case? Most readers will probably recognize these questions. Perceiving the spiritual dimension can be a challenge.

For years I have been active in the deliverance ministry. This helped me enormously in the development of my spiritual senses. I learned that the actual deliverance was taking place in a courtroom. (I will share more about this later.) Because we were pleading in the courts of heaven, we gained a deeper understanding of how the protocols of heaven function. My forty years of military service helped as well. If we want to operate in the courts of heaven successfully, it is vital that we perceive what is happening there.

We need more than an intellectual understanding of the spiritual dimension. After all, that is a function of our soul. As Paul said, we can only perceive and understand what is happening in the spiritual dimension with our spirit.[103] We are able to see that reality with our spiritual eyes. You will know the truth, not because you *heard* someone telling about it, but because you *saw* it with your own eyes.[104]

It is important to perceive the activities in the courts of heaven. Not everyone is a prophet. Not everyone has the office of a seer like Samuel.[105] But we all have received the gift from God to see and to hear in the spiritual dimensions. We can learn to describe exactly what is going on in the courts of heaven. You can use the help of more experienced believers. Don't be discouraged when you read this. This chapter is written especially for you.

---

103 1 Corinthians 2:9-13
104 Job 42:5
105 1 Samuel 9:9

On Earth as It Is in Heaven

Many of us aren't practiced in perceiving what is happening in the spiritual dimensions. But be of good courage, it is our Heavenly Father's desire that we might see Him as He is.[106]

We can use biblical techniques that help us to understand how the heavenly court system is functioning. One of these tools is the awareness that the natural dimension is a shadow and a reflection of the spiritual dimension. We read in Hebrews that the natural things have come forth from the spiritual. We also read that the tabernacle that Moses built on the earth was an exact replica of the tabernacle in heaven.

> *Who serve the copy and shadow of the heavenly things, as Moses was divinely instructed when he was about to make the tabernacle. For He said, "See that you make all things according to the pattern shown you on the mountain.*
>
> *Hebrews 8:5*

> *By faith we understand that the worlds were framed by the word of God, so that the things which are seen were not made of things which are visible.*
>
> *Hebrews 11:3*

It is important to understand that the spiritual dimension is the source, the origin, of the natural dimension. Everything that we see, taste, smell, and experience with our natural senses is a shadow, a copy, of the spiritual dimension. When heaven sees that the protocol and patterns of heaven exist on the earth, then heaven will manifest itself. It is as if heaven is waiting until the earth and heaven become one; then heaven will reveal itself on the earth. As Paul said, we can also reverse this process.

> *If there is a natural body, there is also a spiritual body.*
>
> *1 Corinthians 15:44 (NIV)*

There is a spiritual equivalent for every natural body. But the heart of the matter is that there is no real harmony, no connection, between the natural and the spiritual body. When we search the natural structures and processes on the earth, we are able, together with the Spirit of God, to

---

[106] 1 John 3:2

picture the heavenly dimension because the earthly things are a copy of the spiritual.

What we perceive on the earth is a shadow of the heavenly reality. The instant that the natural body is delivered from the oppression of the evil one, the natural body will be visible in the spiritual dimension. We can see this on the mount of transfiguration. For an instant, the body of Jesus was changed before the eyes of the disciples. His face shone like the sun and His clothes became white as the light.[107]

Seeing the Voice of God

Yes, you are reading this correctly. *Seeing* the voice of God. In recent years, a lot of books have been published about hearing the voice of God. Jesus promised us that we can know the voice of God.[108] Every child of God is capable of recognizing His voice and many of us can testify about this.

But John gives us an important clue in the book of Revelations, due to the position he had. When we are on the earth, we are able to hear the voice of God, but when we are in the heavens, we are able to *see* the voice of God. John was taken up by the Spirit on the day of the Lord.

> *I was in the Spirit on the Lord's Day, and I heard behind me a loud voice, as of a trumpet, saying, "I am the Alpha and the Omega, the First and the Last," and, "What you see, write in a book and send it to the seven churches which are in Asia: to Ephesus, to Smyrna, to Pergamos, to Thyatira, to Sardis, to Philadelphia, and to Laodicea."*
> *Then I turned to see the voice that spoke with me. And having turned I saw seven golden lampstands, and in the midst of the seven lampstands One like the Son of Man, clothed with a garment down to the feet and girded about the chest with a golden band.*
> *Revelation 1:10-13*

It says here that John turned around in order to *see* the voice that had spoken to him. He saw what was going on in the heavenly dimension because he was *in the Spirit*. The book of Revelation is the written record of

---

107 Matthew 17:2
108 John 10:4

his visit to heaven. John was actually present in heaven. The invitation that John received is also available to us. The door is open.

After these things I looked, and behold, a door standing open in heaven. And the first voice which I heard was like a trumpet speaking with me, saying, "Come up here, and I will show you things which must take place after this."

Revelation 4:1

For most of us, it is a real challenge to experience the same things as John did. The greatest hinderances are in our emotions and in our mind. We can more easily pray for another person and receive encouraging words or impressions for them. Sometimes, people surprise us with encouragements that were exactly what we needed. But when we are seeking God for our personal lives, it seems as if our eyes and ears are closed.

Entering the heavenly dimensions is an act of faith
by our spirit.

This could be because we try to enter the spiritual dimensions from our soul, not our spirit. Entering the heavenly dimensions is an act of faith by our spirit. John describes it as something we do with our spirit.

It is important that we cultivate the desire to see and hear the voice of God. When He invites us, it is vital that we respond to Him. Some of us may have the conviction that God isn't speaking anymore, or that He only speaks to a very select and elite group of people.

But nothing can be further from the truth. It is important that we learn how to activate our spiritual senses, in order that we might be able to see and understand the voices that are speaking to us from heaven. Our spiritual eyes are opened by prayer, just as it was done in the life of the servant of Elisha.

Elisha in Dothan

Naaman was a high general in the army of the king of Syria, but Naaman was a leper who came to Israel to be healed. When Naaman arrived before the king of Israel, the king panicked. "Who does he think I am? I am not God. Is Naaman seeking a reason to go to war?"

Elisha hears of this and sends a message to the King of Israel: "Send Naaman to me. He shall know that there is a prophet in Israel."

We all know the end of the story. Naaman is healed from his leprosy and returns to the court of the king of Syria. A few years later, the king of Syria starts a war against the king of Israel.

But the king of Israel outwits his tactics every time, and the king of Syria becomes furious. He is convinced that there are spies in his kingdom that inform the King of Israel of his plans. From that moment on, Naaman must have feared for his life. After all, he was healed in Israel of his leprosy. Perhaps the Syrians would suspect Naaman had made a covenant with the king of Israel in return for his healing.

Fortunately, there was a servant that tells the king of Syria what was really happening. "It is Elisha," he says. "He tells the king of Israel all the words that you speak in your bedroom." Talk about perceiving in the spiritual dimension!

The king of Syria redirects his anger to Elisha, sending his whole army to capture him and bring him to Syria.

Every child of God is capable of recognizing His voice.

During the night, the great Syrian army surrounds the city with horses and chariots. In the morning, the servant of Elisha sees them and becomes terrified. Elisha reassures him and prays that God would open the servant's eyes.

The result is astonishing! The servant sees with his own eyes that the hosts of heaven have surrounded Elisha with horses, chariots, *and fire.* This army was stronger; outnumbering the Syrian army. Elisha prays again and asks the Lord to blind the eyes of the Syrians. This is a miracle; the Syrians can look with their eyes but can't see anything.

So he answered, "Do not fear, for those who are with us are more than those who are with them." And Elisha prayed, and said, "Lord, I pray, open his eyes that he may see." Then the Lord opened the eyes of the young man, and he saw. And behold, the mountain was full of horses and chariots of fire all around Elisha.

2 Kings 6:16-17

In this story we see that prayer opens *and* closes eyes. The Bible often speaks of someone lifting their eyes to the heavens to see things that couldn't be seen by the natural eye. So be aware that we have spiritual eyes and natural eyes. Just as Abraham, Ezekiel, Daniel, and many others saw the heavenly dimensions, we too can perceive the courts of heaven with our spiritual eyes. Now you might wonder: *How can I do this?* I will give you an example.

When you read the Bible, imagine a mental picture of the text you are reading. For example, Scripture tells us that we are surrounded by a great cloud of witnesses. Try to picture yourself standing in the heavenly court-room with thousands of people cheering you on. In order to experience this literally, try going to a stadium. Close your eyes when the home team scores a goal or a touchdown. Listen to the cheering of the public and visualize yourself standing in the courts of heaven. What you experience in that moment in the stadium is also happening in heaven. Everyone stands to support you.

The key in this is to find Jesus or, as it says in Hebrews, to fix your eyes on Jesus.

> *Therefore we also, since we are surrounded by so great a cloud of witnesses, let us lay aside every weight, and the sin which so easily ensnares us, and let us run with endurance the race that is set before us, looking unto Jesus, the author and finisher of our faith, who for the joy that was set before Him endured the cross, despising the shame, and has sat down at the right hand of the throne of God.*
> *Hebrews 12:1-2*

Let us reach out for this spiritual gift that we might be able to perceive correctly what the Judge is telling us and doing for us. Keep your eyes constantly focused on Jesus and not on your enemy—who is totally irrelevant to you.

Opening of Eyes and Ears

Jesus told His disciples that the eyes and ears of the multitudes were closed. The people simply were not able to understand the message of His kingdom. On the other hand, His disciples were so blessed to be chosen to receive the mysteries of the kingdom out of the hands of the Father.

He answered and said to them, "Because it has been given to you to know the mysteries of the kingdom of heaven, but to them it has not been given. Therefore I speak to them in parables because seeing they do not see, and hearing they do not hear, nor do they understand. And in them the prophecy of Isaiah is fulfilled, which says:
"Hearing you will hear and shall not understand, And seeing you will see and not perceive; For the hearts of this people have grown dull. Their ears are hard of hearing, And their eyes they have closed, Lest they should see with their eyes and hear with their ears, Lest they should understand with their hearts and turn, So that I should heal them."
But blessed are your eyes for they see, and your ears for they hear; for assuredly, I say to you that many prophets and righteous men desired to see what you see, and did not see it, and to hear what you hear, and did not hear it.

Matthew 13:11,13-17

In this passage, Jesus gives us keys to open our eyes and ears. Why could the people not hear and see? They had closed their eyes themselves. Their heart had grown dull and they had become spiritually lazy. They weren't interested in searching the Scriptures themselves; they used others to do that. Their walk with God could be compared to a drive-in restaurant. They didn't want to pay the price in order to receive the mysteries of the kingdom.

Hearing and seeing in the spiritual dimension are not gifts reserved for the happy few. They are available for every true disciple of Jesus, not for those who choose to stay in the multitudes. Understanding the words of Jesus and perceiving in the spiritual dimensions are directly connected with your personal devotion to Him. Every person is called to be a disciple of Jesus, but not everyone is willing to pay the price. Those who do are the real chosen ones of the Lord. They are initiated in the mysteries of the kingdom of heaven.

The disciples left their homes and their families. They renounced their natural inheritances. They left wives and children in order to follow Him, not knowing how it would end. Too many Christians want their blessing to be presented on a plate. They want to be served in a restaurant where everything is free.

But there is always a price to pay when you follow Jesus. Jesus tells His listeners that they must change the way they think so that they might hear and see again. Just like the disciples, we also must pay a price. Becoming a mature son or daughter of God has everything to do with taking up your responsibilities.

And whoever does not bear his cross and come after Me cannot be My disciple. So likewise, whoever of you does not forsake all that he has cannot be My disciple.

Luke 14:27,33

Blessed Are the Pure In Heart, Because They Will See God

This is what Jesus tells His disciples in the sermon on the mount.[109] We are living in a time where it is difficult to live a pure and holy life. But the promise that Jesus gives here is so encouraging. When our heart is pure, then shall we see our God! That is our challenge: the purification of our heart; the seat of our thought life. It is under enormous pressure.

Hearing and seeing in the spiritual dimension
are not gifts reserved for the happy few.

Who hasn't struggled with pornography and its consequences in their life? Don't assume that struggling with sexuality is typically a male problem. Women can also use their imaginations in a wrong way in order to be satisfied in their soul. The results are that our hearts become wounded and we lose sight of the heavenly realities.

It isn't only the sex that makes our hearts impure, but also listening to those who speak ill over other people.

The words of a talebearer are like tasty trifles, and they go down into the inmost body.

Proverbs 18:8

The book of Proverbs is a great manual for a pure and holy life. You can't imagine how much is being said about our physical senses. In my Bible, I have marked every verse that talks about our eyes, mouth, ears, hands,

---

[109] Matthew 5:8

or feet. It was a big surprise for me when I discovered how much is said about our body in the book of Proverbs. Seeing and hearing in the spiritual dimension is a process; partially in our heart and partially in our brain.

Because of this, it is critically important to cleanse our heart and our mind of all the bad images and words with the blood of Jesus. Mind you, this is not a process that will be completed in a single day.

One way to cleanse our body and our soul is to read one chapter of Proverbs every day out loud and meditate over it. There are 31 chapters in this extraordinary book, and we can study a chapter a day. Constantly ask the Holy Spirit to help you in the cleansing of your heart and mind. Over time, you will experience the ability to perceive more and more of the spiritual dimension.

Learning How to See in The Spiritual Dimensions

While praying for the Ephesians, Paul asked that the eyes of their understanding might be opened. That is their spiritual eyes. It was his desire that they would perceive the greatness of the plan of God for their lives with their own eyes. To God, it is of the utmost importance that we learn how to see; that the eyes of our hearts and of our minds might be opened.

> ... that the God of our Lord Jesus Christ, the Father of glory, may give to you the spirit of wisdom and revelation in the knowledge of Him, the eyes of your understanding being enlightened; that you may know what is the hope of His calling, what are the riches of the glory of His inheritance in the saints, and what is the exceeding greatness of His power toward us who believe, according to the working of His mighty power, ...
>
> Ephesians 1:17-19

The spiritual dimension becomes very real the moment we enter it by faith. We are able to perceive the things that are happening there. But if our eyes are closed, our perceptions are shut.

That is why Paul is praying this prayer. As long as we cannot see our position in Christ, the enemy will have the upper hand. As long as we choose to live our lives from the flesh, our eyes will remain closed. That is the real reason why it is so important to be led by the Spirit[110] and why we must activate our spiritual senses. Let's meditate on this verse in Ephesians until we really understand and grasp the meaning of it.

But there is more. The enemy's real goal is to keep us blinded as long as possible. Paul says that the god of this age has blinded the eyes of the people. Their natural eyes are open, but they can't perceive the glory and the greatness of Jesus Christ.[111] Once our eyes are opened, we will be able to see the richness and the glory that God has prepared for us. Then we shall be able to hear and see what God is saying to us. When we present our case in the heavenly courts, we will be able to perceive and understand what is happening there.

Conclusion

It is God's desire that we all see Him as He is. It is the enemy who has blinded our spiritual eyes. As with any other spiritual gift, the initiative to develop it lies in our hands. It is we who must come into action. It is we who ought to be successful in the courts of heaven. Jesus has promised us that we shall see God, as long as our hearts and our minds are pure. Devote yourself to the purification of your heart.

But this is a process, not a quick fix. Develop a disciplined lifestyle. I encourage you to read books that enable you to develop your spiritual sight[112] so that you become able to perceive the spiritual dimension. Over time, you will know when your spiritual eyes are opened, and you will perceive more and more of that beautiful dimension.

For you have need of endurance, so that after you have done the will of God, you may receive the promise.

Hebrews 10:36

I will discuss the protocol and the code of conduct in the courts of heaven in the next chapter.

---

[110] Romans 8:1-2
[111] 2 Corinthians 4:4
[112] *The Seer*, by James Goll, Destiny Image, 2004
The School of the Seers, by Jonathan Welton, Destiny Image, 2009

10

Courtroom Protocols

When you present your case in an earthly courtroom, you must follow the proper protocol. There are specific codes of conduct that everyone should obey. All these rules and procedures are specified and written down. The Judge can order you to be removed from the courtroom if you don't comply with these regulations. Everybody must obey them, whether you are a suspect, a prosecutor, a visitor, or even a judge. During a court session, the orderly development is closely monitored.

Most of us have seen television shows about a court session that became emotional. A good example is in the movie *A Few Good Men*, starring Tom Cruise and Jack Nicholson. The plot is simple but exciting. A young marine was found dead in his bed the morning after his fellow marines applied a punitive measure, nicknamed "Code Red." The base commander tried to sweep the case under the rug. The marines who carried out the "Code Red" were put on trial, in order to be convicted. But this plan seemed doomed when the lead attorney (Lieutenant Daniel Kaffee), a notorious deal-maker, decided to take on the case.

During the cross-examination by Daniel Kaffee, the base commander, Colonel Nathan Jessup, became enraged at the Judged because Daniel was not treating him with proper respect. The Judge ordered Daniel to address the commander with the proper title: Colonel. The Colonel was so frustrated that he barked at the Judge: "I don't know what the hell kind of unit you're running here."

The judge snapped back at him: "And the witness will address this court as 'Judge' or 'Your Honor.' I'm quite certain *I've* earned it. Take your seat, Colonel."

This is just one example of how the court protocol works. There is always proper respect given to each party that is present during the court session. The judge stands above all parties and functions as a chairman. The clerk is always silent but registers everything that happens. The lawyers can address the judge or the jury, but only after the judge has allowed them to do so.

The same is true in a criminal case where the prosecutor represents the state. All those who are present are educated in the law and have taken their bar exam. They are licensed and sworn in to fulfill their formal role in the proceedings. In some nations, they all wear black robes, which shows that they have a formal capacity and privileges. These roles and privileges are to be respected by everyone in the courtroom.

Deliverance in A Courtroom Setting

My first experiences with the deliverance ministry were in a traditional Pentecostal church. They used the common Pentecostal method for deliverance, as did every other Pentecostal church in those days. There was a lot of shouting, not only by the Christians, but especially by the demons. The person we prayed for rolled on the ground, vomited, and literally screamed as one possessed. Perhaps you have seen these kinds of prayers on YouTube.

But when we were introduced to new ideas for deliverance ministry in the late 90s, many things changed. One of the most remarkable changes was the respect we showed during the sessions. There was no more screaming and vomiting; not by demons or humans. What appealed to me personally was how much the Father loved and respected His children. The client was sitting comfortably on his chair and wasn't humiliated by the demons anymore. But the respect wasn't only for the client. The demons also were treated with a form of respect because they were subpoenaed *in the courts of heaven.*

When we began these new approaches, many Christians were against this type of ministry. They found it outrageous, saying, "You ought not to show the devil any respect. He must be humiliated and destroyed."

But they didn't understand the difference between showing someone respect in a courtroom and honoring someone. We don't honor demons during a court session, but we honor the court's protocol because we are in the courtroom of the eternal Judge. This is where the difference lies. The adversaries of the Holy Ones of God are standing on trial for all the atrocities they have done in the life of a child of God.

We are not screaming in the courtroom—not on earth nor in heaven. Demons aren't deaf; they have very good hearing. We don't curse them; we hold them responsible for everything they have done. We ask God, the eternal Judge, to render a verdict that is consistent with the atrocities they have performed. This is the way that we judge them just as Ezekiel did when he judged Oholah and Oholibah.

> The Lord also said to me: "Son of man, will you judge Oholah and Oholibah? Then declare to them their abominations. For they have committed adultery, and blood is on their hands."
>
> Ezekiel 23:36,37

This is our assignment in the courts of heaven. We judge the enemies of our God by making public all the things they have performed in secret. Because we present the evidence in the courts of heaven for the things these demons did, God the Judge is able to render a verdict over them. The enemy doesn't want the veils removed that block his activities from the public sight because everyone will then be able to see who he really is.[113]

The Respect for The Office

We all have seen these shows on television where the court clerk commands everybody to stand when the judge enters the courtroom: "All rise!" This is a standard protocol, but it can be different in other nations. In the Netherlands, the clerk says, "The court!"

A few years ago, there was a case in the Netherlands where a lawyer refused to stand as the judge entered the courtroom.[114] The lawyer was brought to justice (ultimately, his license to practice law was revoked), entirely because of his failure to comply with the court's protocol.

The reason this lawyer didn't want to rise for the judge is quite significant. He held a personal opinion that, according to his faith, all men are equal. To his mind, the judge was no exception to this rule. What this lawyer probably didn't understand was that we don't rise for the person of the judge, but for the office of the judge. We rise for the position, the power, and the authority that the office of judge represents. When we

---

[113] Isaiah 14:16
[114] https://nl.wikipedia.org/wiki/Mohammed_Enait

rise, we show respect for the office of the judge and the institution of the court.

When we are driving a car and the police officer signals us to stop, we pull over, right? Even if the police officer is a young 23-year-old man, we obey him. Why? Because he represents the authority of the state or government. This is the same reason we stand when our national anthem is being sung. It is a sign of respect to the national anthem and what it represents, regardless of the people who are currently in office.

The protocols in the courts of heaven aren't much different than the ones on the earth. You can't enter a court and just start presenting your case. You must first be given the proper authority to do that. Fortunately, we have received this right to enter the mobile court any time we want to. But that doesn't mean that there are no protocols we are obligated to follow.

The fact that the enemy has caused tremendous damage in our lives weighs heavy for our Judge.

Before we begin presenting our case in court, we first show respect to the Judge and those who are present in court. We do this by honoring Him and asking Him to open the court session. If the court is not in session, then no verdict can be rendered. At the moment that the session is opened, the books are opened also.

The court was seated, and the books were opened.

Daniel 7:10

The opening of these books is essential. It is impossible to read or write in a book when it is closed. It sounds simple and it is. It is also crucial that everything that happens during a court session is recorded. Everything that is recorded can be brought into evidence during the pleadings. In every formal court session, there is a clerk present (also called the *scriba* in Latin), who writes everything down that is happening.

Respecting the Court

It is important for us to recognize the authority of the heavenly court, and we have to speak it out loud. If we don't recognize the court, we can't present our case there.

Then we tell the Judge why we appear before Him. We don't appear in court to prove ourselves right. We appear in court in order to fight for justice and to fight the injustice that has tried to hinder us in realizing the assignment that God has given us. We don't plead in order to lift ourselves up, but we plead for the honor of the King of Kings. We are in court to honor Him, not to be contentious, and to stop the hindering of the fulfillment of destinies.

> *But if anyone seems to be contentious, we have no such custom, nor do the churches of God.*
>
> 1 Corinthians 11:16

We show respect to everyone who is present during the court session. Much more is happening there than we realize. For instance, there are more than 100 million creatures before the throne: the witnesses, the spirit of people made righteous who are in heaven, and the angels. The enemy is also present, sometimes with an entourage. But they all show respect because *we are in a court.*

The Judge doesn't rule based on His emotions. He renders a verdict based on the evidence, facts, and all the testimonies that are presented during the court session.

The fact that the enemy has caused tremendous damage in our lives weighs heavy for our Judge. When I state that a court session is emotionless, this doesn't mean that emotions are not weighed into consideration. Sorrow, pain, and intense trauma are definitely a factor of the verdict of the Judge. But His ruling is not based on His emotions or ours for that matter. They are based on His righteousness and His justice. We don't receive preferential treatment. When someone is found guilty as charged, they will be convicted and receive his punishment.

> *God is jealous, and the Lord avenges; the Lord avenges and is furious. The Lord will take vengeance on His adversaries, and He reserves wrath for His enemies;*

the Lord is slow to anger and great in power, and will not at all acquit the wicked.

Nahum 1:2

We Address the Judge

When we present our case, we address the judge and not our adversary. A friend of mine was a material witness in a court session in a Middle Eastern nation. He was asked to give his expert opinion about the delivery of a construction project. There were several parties present during the court session. The plaintiff stated that the constructed building didn't comply with the contract. There was also a defendant, who argued that everything was fine.

My friend was seated to the right before the judge. To his left and right were the attorneys of both parties. When one of the lawyers of the plaintiff asked him a question, my friend turned to his right side to answer him. But the judge immediately intervened, instructing my friend to give his answer to the judge directly.

Similarly, we see this in the Netherlands' national parliament. Every speaker addresses the chairman. They talk *about* the government and *about* the other members of parliament, but they do not address them personally.

We see this also in the courts of heaven. We don't wage a war of words with our adversary. We address the Heavenly Judge and present our case *to Him*. We place the verdict about our case into His hands. We also ask for compensation for the things that were done to us, or unto those on whose behalf we are standing there. Of course, we can express our emotions, but we do this to our Father, the Judge of all the earth. He will render a verdict in a just way.

Satan Wants to Declare Us Inadmissible

When we appear in the courts of heaven before the Judge, satan will try to do anything to silence us in the court. He knows that when the Judge rules in our favor, his power on the earth will be broken. He tries to motion for the Judge to declare our case inadmissible. This almost happened with the high priest Joshua. He appeared before the angel of the Lord, and satan was standing at his side to oppose him.

Then he showed me Joshua the high priest standing before the Angel of the Lord, and satan standing at his right hand to oppose him. And the Lord said to Satan, "The Lord rebuke you, Satan! The Lord who has chosen Jerusalem rebuke you! Is this not a brand plucked from the fire?" Now Joshua was clothed with filthy garments, and was standing before the Angel.

Zechariah 3:1-2

Joshua had entered the heavenlies to stand in the gap for his nation. When Zechariah saw this vision, he probably saw Joshua entering the Holy of Holies on the day of Yom Kippur, the Day of Atonement. The high priest offered the blood of the lamb, in order to atone for the sins of the nation.

But satan wanted to prevent his sacrifice from being accepted in heaven. Satan began to accuse the one who brought the offering---Joshua. He wanted a motion to rule Joshua's offering as inadmissible. He does this by pointing to the dirty garments of Joshua the high priest. In Scripture, our garments are symbolically referring to our righteous deeds.[115] When they are dirty, the person has unrighteousness in his life.

When we are in the courts of heaven, it is the Judge who rebukes satan, not us.

But the angel of the LORD parries the accusations and rebukes satan. He himself stands in the gap for Jerusalem. He says to him: "The Lord will rebuke you, satan!" He leaves the verdict over satan in the hands of God Himself.

There is an important lesson to learn here. When we are in the courts of heaven, it is the Judge who rebukes satan. Not even the angel of the Lord, or an archangel, does it.

You address the Heavenly Judge and you leave the rebuke to Him; He will deal with the accusations that satan presents in court. We must not become irrational, foolish slanderers, who from powerlessness and

---

[115] Revelation 19:8

frustration speak all kinds of foolish things against satan and his powers. Let us learn from the archangel Michael, who didn't rebuke satan.

> *Yet Michael the archangel, in contending with the devil, when he disputed about the body of Moses, dared not bring against him a reviling accusation, but said, "The Lord rebuke you!" But these speak evil of whatever they do not know; and whatever they know naturally, like brute beasts, in these things they corrupt themselves.*
>
> *Jude 1:9-10*

The unrighteousness of Joshua is dealt with by giving him new garments. Did you notice that Joshua didn't speak one word during all of this? When we are in the heavenly courts, other voices will speak on our behalf. Even the prophet Zechariah gave an order here.

It is not necessary to speak all the time. When satan accuses you, God will give us a new garment when we walk in humility and meekness, appearing humbly before Him. Joshua wasn't appearing in the heavenly court for himself, but he entered to atone for the sins of a nation, in order that Israel might fulfill her destiny on the earth.

Righteousness and Justice

The power and the authority of the kingdom of heaven are based on the righteous respect and application of its laws and regulations. The Bible tells us that the foundation of the throne of God is righteousness and justice.[116] If God would give us preference in His court, He would break His own laws. At that instant, the accuser would accuse God of partiality. That will never happen. God has given us strict instructions on how the court's application of the law in Israel must be fulfilled.

> *You shall not circulate a false report. Do not put your hand with the wicked to be an unrighteous witness. You shall not follow a crowd to do evil; nor shall you testify in a dispute so as to turn aside after many to pervert justice. You shall not show partiality to a poor man in his dispute. If you meet your enemy's ox or his donkey going astray, you shall surely bring it back to him again.*

---

[116] Psalm 89:14; Psalm 97:2

If you see the donkey of one who hates you lying under its burden, and you would refrain from helping it, you shall surely help him with it. You shall not pervert the judgment of your poor in his dispute. Keep yourself far from a false matter; do not kill the innocent and righteous. For I will not justify the wicked. And you shall take no bribe, for a bribe blinds the discerning and perverts the words of the righteous.

Exodus 23:1-8

In this passage, we come to understand that people can't see properly when they accept a bribe and pervert words. If, despite all your efforts, you still struggle with seeing in the spiritual dimension, ask the Holy Spirit if this is the reason why you are not yet able to see. It could be that one of your ancestors has given a false testimony or took a bribe, in order to get an innocent man convicted. The enemy uses the laws and regulations from God to hinder us. Satan will accuse us—trying to keep us blinded as long as he can—and he uses God's commandments to do so.

Conclusion

God the Judge has laid down rules of conduct for proper protocol in the courts. These rules are not only applicable in an earthly court, but also in the heavenly courts. When we enter His courts for our personal cases, we won't be punished when we make a mistake. Before His throne He will give us mercy, not only for what we have done on the earth but also for our lack of understanding of proper protocol.

Our Father is really excited when we appear before Him in order to bring justice to the earth. When we do, we allow Him to speak justice into our lives and to bless us, so that He can give us what He desires for us. But be aware that our God is not a God of chaos but of order.[117]

This ends the biblical foundation for operating in the courts of heaven. In the second part of this book, I will discuss the practical application. I will help you with the different steps you can take in this process, so that you may be able to present your case before the Judge over all the earth.

---

[117] 1 Corinthians 14:33

Part 2:

Practical Application

11

Well-Begun Is...

We are all different; fortunately. We all have our own habits and peculiarities. That is the charm of being a human being. Some people have the habit of reading Part 1 of this book first, before they start with Part 2. Others skip that whole idea and go straight to Part 2; the practical application. These are the same people that open the box and immediately begin using the new appliances, while others take the time to read the user manual first. (There must be a reason why it's in there, right?) In most cases, that is just fine. You can skip reading the large manual that came with your new television. There isn't much that could go wrong, other than missing out on a few cool functions. You'll most likely discover them eventually, even if it takes a couple of years.

But in this case, I want to urge you to read the first part of this book before you start entering the courts of heaven. Your mind will receive a new level of understanding so that you're well prepared. The courts of heaven are real! The verdict is binding on all parties. It is important to have some background about the courts of heaven, so that we understand the protocol and we know what our mandate is.

Our adversary is not impressed by our reputation on the earth. Think about the sons of Sceva and what happened to them.[118] They were itinerant Jewish exorcists who thought they could use the name of Jesus as a new tool in their toolbox against some evil spirits. But they were pounded without mercy.

We can learn some valuable lessons from this. When you think you can beat your adversary in the courts of heaven just because you have heard of the existence of it, you are gravely mistaken. It is a spiritual dimension; everyone there sees right through you. It is impossible to hide behind your reputation. Every thought you have, every deed you've done, and every word spoken are fully displayed and open on the table. Our adversary is a roaring lion seeking whom he can devour. Reading the first

---

[118] Acts 19:13-20

part of this book is a good preparation so that we can say like Paul: "We are not ignorant of his devices."[119]

Wonderful Counselor

Many of us have never personally seen the inside of a courtroom. What we know about the court is what we learned from others or from shows on television. We only enter a courtroom when it is our profession or when we are involved in a court case.

But we can all understand that good preparation is very important. It all starts with a conversation with your lawyer. You talk about what is going to happen from the beginning of the trial until the end of it. Thankfully, we too have a wonderful Counselor who helps us in the preparation of our heavenly court case.[120] The Spirit of Counsel will also stand at our side and help us with the preparation of our case. Don't hesitate to prayerfully ask His help.

Our adversary is not impressed by our reputation on the earth.

Preparing your case means that you think about which position you will take and consider how your opponent will react to that. You try to anticipate his moves. You ensure that your pleas are based on the promises of God in the Bible. You consider all the important facts. Your witnesses are capable to support your plea with their testimonies. You even consider the arguments your opponent can bring into the case, and you prepare yourself to answer his arguments and prove him wrong. You don't want to be tongue-tied, do you?

When you haven't prepared your case, it could mean that you will lose the case, even if you can prove afterward that you were right all the time. The Heavenly Judge can't render His verdict based on His love and feelings for you. He rules based on the facts, the evidence, and the statements that are presented during the court session. When the verdict is rendered, new evidence can no longer easily change the verdict.

---

[119] 2 Corinthians 2:11
[120] Isaiah 9:6

Roe v. Wade

Let me give an example. Most of you have probably heard of the case Roe versus Wade. It was a landmark decision by the United States Supreme Court in 1973. The Court ruled on the abortion laws that existed in many states at that time. The Court decided that most laws that prohibited abortions or restricted them were unconstitutional. The Court ruled that the right for an abortion was covered by the constitutional right of privacy. The abortion laws were lifted in every state across the US. Even today, this ruling is one of the most controversial rulings in the history of the United States Supreme Court.[121]

What were the consequences of this ruling? At the time of writing this book, in the United States alone 60,942,033 children have been murdered; slaughtered in utero.[122] That is *sixty million nine-hundred and forty-two thousand and thirty three* scrolls that are not being fulfilled! Try to imagine this number as living people and you can fill many nations of the earth with them! I am convinced that God's enemy, satan, won this court case because we as Christian weren't standing in the gap for the nation. The verdict was rendered in favor of the enemy of God. You can't turn that around again. Can you imagine what this meant for the heart of our Father when He as Judge had to render this verdict? He couldn't do anything but meet the demands of satan.

The Bible sometimes says that the Lord causes a plague. God doesn't want to cause a plague, but He is bound by the protocol of His own Court and the laws of His kingdom. He can't change it when He presides as Judge in the courts of heaven. He can't change His verdict, even when the outcome hurts Him. This is why the Lord becomes upset when He finds that no one is standing in the gap for the nation.

> *So I sought for a man among them who would make a wall, and stand in the gap before Me on behalf of the land, that I should not destroy it; but I found no one.*
>
> *Ezekiel 22:30*

When no one appears in court to plead for a nation, a district, or a city, the Judge can't do anything else but to allow His enemy to activate a

---

[121] https://en.wikipedia.org/wiki/Roe_v._Wade
[122] https://christianliferesources.com/beginning-of-life/abortion/ (2019-04-18)

curse. I can hear some of you already arguing: "But isn't Jesus pleading for our nation in heaven?"

Yes, that's true, but to render a verdict, there must be two or three witnesses. In order to render a verdict in heaven, there must be witnesses on earth that testify together with Christ in heaven.

John tells us in Revelations that the spirit of prophecy is the testimony of Jesus.[123] When Jesus is testifying, He encourages us to be His fellow witnesses. We do this by letting our voice be heard in the courts of heaven and through our prophecy on the earth. Earth and heaven must become one, in order to give the verdict of heaven legal force on the earth.

But you might ask: If this is true, who then is testifying on the earth on behalf of satan? You will be surprised to hear that the strongest testimonies that support the cases of satan in the courts of heaven are the testimonies that we Christians give. When we speak badly about a person, or slander or gossip about our brother or leader in church, then our testimony is recorded in heaven. We may keep silent in total indifference about the things that occur in society, believing that Jesus will return soon and save us from our society. Let us be aware of the responsibilities we as sons of God carry and are called to fulfill.

Fixed Components of a Court Case

During every court session, there are fixed components. In order to help you to present your case, the steps you need to take are described in the following chapters.

Before you start with the preparation of your case, it is important to know and understand your identity and your position. Do you really know who you are when you are in heaven? This is why you must begin to explore your own scroll. When you know what your God-given assignment is, you also know what your mandate in the courts of heaven is.

Then you describe what injustice has been done to you. Describe which is your part and what part your opponent played in the conflict. You ask forgiveness for the mistakes that you have made, and you bless the people who have hurt you. I want to emphasize again that forgiveness

---

[123] Revelation 19:10

is a legal action, not the consequence of an emotion. Our emotions demand instant retribution, but when we forgive others, we place the right for retaliation in the hands of the Righteous Judge. He will judge with righteous judgment.

You gather evidence and call in the witnesses. You start pleading your case according to the promises that are in the Bible. Then you formulate your charges and the compensation you want to receive. You present this all to your Father, the Judge. The Judge will render a verdict and you will receive the written judgment from Him. The divorce papers are also signed. You will bring this written judgment to the earth and you begin executing everything written in it. In short, these are the steps we take during the whole trial.

When you have never been to a heavenly court, you won't have a frame of reference. That is why the first time can be difficult. Don't hesitate to ask more experienced persons to help with this. But realize that a court session, on earth and in heaven, is serious business. The verdict of the Judge is binding for all parties, even if you have expected a different ruling.

Be at peace. When you start pleading in the courts of heaven for the first time, there is a lot of grace for you. You are supported by many helpers and comforters.

Know that the Heavenly Judge is always merciful toward His children. The most important thing is the attitude of your heart. When you are honestly trying to correct a wrong, the Judge won't dismiss you when you make a mistake because you are trying your best. After all, He is still your Father and your Friend. Jesus is standing at your side as your Advocate. When you act in the spirit of love, that grace will be your ally, even if you don't follow protocol as you should have. But if you make a half-hearted attempt and assume it will be all right in the end, you will be held in contempt of the court. Your charge won't be accepted; not on the earth and not in heaven.

Ownership Is Important

Earlier in this book, I stated that we enter a lawsuit in heaven when we pray for deliverance. One of the important principles here is that the client is responsible for what goes on in his own life. When the confidant who receives their deliverance doesn't take responsibility for their own life, praying for them is useless.

The same is true when we pray in the courts of heaven. You must own your responsibility for your life. There will always be people that are able to help you, especially when you start praying like this for the first time. But you are responsible for the preparation, the investigation, the gathering of evidence, defining the charges, and asking forgiveness of the people you have hurt during the conflict.

You will receive many assignments in the coming chapters. Do your homework; it will benefit you. There is a workbook available that can assist you in preparing your case.[124] The assignments and prayers there are developed to help you; we will discuss this more in the coming chapters.

> The main purpose of these proceedings is that
> the will of God is established on earth,
> as it is in the heavens.

When you receive a revelation about your own scroll, write it down. This applies to all the assignments: Write down the Bible verses that you want to use in the workbook. When you write these verses also in your heart, no one will be able to take them away. When you do this for the first time, it can take you a while before you are ready. But don't let this keep you from the fulfillment of the desires of your heart, in order to receive your justice in the courts of heaven.

The courts of heaven are not a quick fix for our problems; these trials are held in the courts of heaven to give you justice. Sometimes you receive an answer or a verdict that you didn't expect. Just like in a court on earth, the verdict of our Heavenly Judge can surprise you. The main purpose of these proceedings is that the will of God is established on earth, as it is in the heavens. The courts of heaven are an integral part of the kingdom of the heavens.

Your destiny and the realization of your dreams are interconnected with the plan of God for your life. When we are successful in the realization of our destinies, the whole of creation will also be restored. Creation

---

[124] Workbook Courts of Heaven for Beginners, Publishing House Seferim, 2019.

is suffering under the regime of a ruthless enemy who has no respect for anything or anyone. It is our duty to stand in the gap and present our case in the courts of heaven.

> *For the earnest expectation of the creation eagerly waits for the revealing of the sons of God.*
>
> *Romans 8:19*

Conclusion

Well begun is half done. This is especially true when you are preparing your court case. When you start exploring and moving more and more in the heavenly dimension, you will discover that it becomes easier. And yes, you must pull out all the stops. But isn't that the characteristic of maturity, that you are capable of carrying your responsibility?

Put your fears aside. There is so much grace for you. The Father is longing that you will stand in the gap for righteousness and justice on the earth; first in our own lives, then in our cities, districts, states, and nations.

In the next chapter you will find out what is written in *your* scroll, and yes, you are going to find out yourself.

12

What is Written in My Scroll?

Perhaps you have asked yourself this question when you heard about the scrolls of heaven. It is a very good question to ask. A lot of people are thinking about this. Perhaps they are not using words like *scroll* or *courtroom* but they think about their purpose in life and how to fulfill the assignment that God has given them. You will receive some practical tools in this chapter that will enable you to gain some answers to this important question.

Some people know early in life what they are going to achieve. Others have no clue whatsoever; their purpose in life is a great mystery. They are not sure what they are supposed to do in this life; uncertain about what the will of God is for them. This means that making right choices is difficult for them, not because they don't know how to make a choice, but they have no clue why they are on the earth. If that is you, there is hope! God didn't abandon you, but your scroll has been sealed so you are unaware of what is written in it.

The Scroll in the Bible

Why are we on the earth? Many of us might not find this question so easy to answer. When you answer it, you are defining the reason for your existence on earth. In it lies the rationale of one's existence---personally, corporately, or even for a nation. When you don't do what you are called to do, you will probably end up doing the wrong things, and somewhere deep inside you are aware of it. This is why so many are unhappy. They have no clue what to do with their lives.

When we read the vision Isaiah had when he was called by the Lord,[125] we receive some insight into the manner by which our calling is established. Isaiah saw himself standing in the throne room of God. He was overwhelmed by everything he perceived there. Soon, he found out that

---

[125] Isaiah 6:1-13

he was not worthy to be standing there, which is why he cried out: "Woe is me, for I am undone!" His lips were unclean, and his eyes saw the King, the Lord of Hosts. He was being cleansed by the seraphim with a coal from the altar. His sin was purged and his iniquity was taken away. Then he hears the voice of the Lord saying:

"Whom shall I send, and who will go for Us?" Then I said, "Here am I! Send me."

Isaiah 6:8

It is my belief that Isaiah was taken back in time to the moment that the destinies of humanity were being established in the council of the Lord. This happened before God began creating all things. Didn't Jesus say that He glorifies God by doing the works that God had prepared *from the foundation of the world*?[126]

Isaiah stood in the council of the Lord and the Father had an assignment that had to be established on the earth. He asked those who were present there with Him: "Who is willing to do this?" Then He waited until someone answered Him. It was Isaiah who answered this question and received instructions on how to do it (verses 9-13).

I imagine that afterward, Isaiah was led to the scribes where he received a scroll containing the assignment he had just accepted. Then the Father sent him to the earth in order to fulfill it. He received everything he needed to be successful in carrying out his assignment. Everything was adjusted to what was written in his scroll: his personality, his talents, passions, interests, and even the time in which he was born. When Isaiah came out of heaven to the earth, he arrived with a scroll in his belly.[127]

Just like Isaiah, Jeremiah also received his calling before he came to the earth. He also received a clear assignment from God. David had the same experience. He even wrote a complete Psalm about this experience in order to make clear how God was aware of it all. He knows everything, even the beginning.[128] The point is that satan, too, is capable of reading the scrolls of humanity. He doesn't want any of us to be successful in establishing our God-given assignment.

---

[126] John 17:4; Hebrews 4:3
[127] Revelations 10:9-10
[128] Jeremiah 1:4-10; Psalm 139

That is why he is doing everything he can to hinder us when we work out our destinies. He is hindering you too. He seals your scroll with curses and causes you to experience traumas so that you give up. He tries to destroy your faith and affects your memory so you can't remember anything you and the Father have agreed upon.

That is why so many of us walk aimlessly through life like sheep that have no shepherd; lost in the issues of the day. But fortunately, this can all be changed. When you become aware of your assignment---when you have read your scroll---you will be able to be successful in life. Let us, therefore, declare as Nehemiah did:

> So I answered them, and said to them, "The God of heaven Himself will prosper us; therefore we His servants will arise and build, but you have no heritage or right or memorial in Jerusalem."
>
> Nehemiah 2:20

The Sealed Scroll

Scrolls can be sealed and sometimes satan is responsible for it. It can happen when an ancestor has made a covenant with satan. As compensation, satan will receive the legal right to seal the scroll of future generations with curses. It is important to examine your bloodline to see if your ancestors made covenants with the evil one. It could also be that your scroll is sealed because of your own words, or the words of your family, teachers, or church leaders.

So, this question must be answered first. In order to find an answer, do the following: ask the Spirit of Revelation if your ancestors have made a covenant that influences your scroll. You could also ask your family members to tell you about your family history. Did people die prematurely? What habits are dominant in your family? Are people addicted? Do they behave unnaturally? All of these questions can help you gain insight if and how satan is influencing your life.

When it is difficult to find an answer yourself, you can ask others to pray for you. You could ask someone that is familiar with *Restoring the Foundations* prayer to assist you. These teams help to cleanse the foundations in your life. Doing the research about your ancestry is part of the prayer.[129] Breaking the power of ancient curses is something that we do in the courts of heaven.

When you have discovered which seals are on your scroll, isn't it time to remove them? After all, a scroll that is sealed can't be read. We see that John is weeping because no one in heaven was able to break the seals on the scroll in heaven. But his tears made it possible for the Lamb of God to come forward to break these seals.[130] Seals are broken when we have great remorse over our sins and the sins of our ancestors.

Seals are broken also by our obedience. A friend of mine recently discovered the existence of his scroll, but soon found out that it was sealed. When he prayerfully asked the Father what he could do about it, God answered him that he should be baptized. When he did that, one of the seals on his scroll would be broken.

Ask Jesus which seals you can break off your scroll.

Some find it difficult to be baptized in water--not because they aren't convinced it is necessary, but because they find the consequences difficult. When you are baptized, it can have a great effect on the relationships within your family. This is the moment where your obedience is tested. Do you really want to know what is written in your scroll and the assignment God gave to you? Then, obey Him when He asks you to do something, even when it is difficult.

Satan Comes to Destroy

In the many deliverance sessions we have had in the last twenty years, the fun part is always when we begin to unlock the destiny of the confidants we prayed for. The enemy does everything he can to destroy our destinies. The pattern we observe is almost always the same.

The main goal of the hostility that we experience has only one purpose: to destroy one's destiny. When someone was called to be an evangelist, that person would experience agoraphobia. When someone was called to preach, they would stutter. We can use these tactics of the

---

[129] For information please visit: https://www.restoringthefoundations.org/
[130] Revelation 5:1-6

enemy for our benefit in order to get some insight into the calling of God on your life.

This is the reason Revelation tells us of the rewards for those who overcome their enemy. Yes, you can experience fear when you try to step into your destiny. But, the only way to overcome this is to confront it. This is the moment you ask for help in this process from the Holy Spirit of Might.

Describe the greatest battle you had
to fight in your life.

Describe the resistance and the emotions you experience in the battles in your life. Confront the enemies and proclaim the blood of the Lamb. When this question in your life is answered, you will receive the insight of the direction God has given you. Write down what hindrances you have experienced in your life, then match each and every one with a biblical promise from God for your life. Proclaim them daily!

Our Personality Is A Gift

Your personality is created by God to help you be successful in the realization of your assignment. This is why it is important to understand what your personality is, so you can discern its weaknesses and strengths. There are many tests available that can help you to discover what personality you have. The DISC test is just one example.

The DISC test discerns between four personalities types. The first discernment is based on being task-oriented or people-oriented. The second discernment has to do with your decision-making capacity: Do you decide quickly or do you decide over time? The test helps you understand the pitfalls and strengths of each personality. It also helps you to understand if your behavior is the result of your circumstances or the result of your inner strength.

The result of the test is often a combination of two or three personality styles. The first style is the "Dominant Personality," the second style is the "Influential Personality," the third style is the "Steadiness Personality," and the fourth is the "Conscientiousness Personality". In the following table, you see a very simple illustration of the main characteristics of each style.

Simple Presentation DISC Personality Styles

	Dominant	**Influential**
Ideal World	Full of challenges	Having fun
Greatest fear	Loss of control	Rejection
Time focus	It has to happen now	Tomorrow is fine
Emotions	Having a temper	Happiness / Optimism
Question type	What?	Who?
Motivation	Being important	Being recognized
	Conscientious-ness	**Steadiness**
Ideal World	Everything is perfect	Everything is peaceful
Greatest fear	Be criticized	Loss of security
Time focus	Lives in the past	Lives in the present
Emotions	Frightened and careful	Concerned
Question type	Why?	How?
Motivation	Be sure	Building relations

Let's review the terms in the first column on the left. What does your ideal world look like? In other words, which environmental factors are giving you energy? What is your greatest fear, or what are you really afraid of? What is your time focus? Within what time frame are you living? Do you want everything now, or are you always looking to the past? How do you express your emotions? What kind of questions do you ask others or yourself? And finally, what is your biggest motivator in working with others?

Find out which personality describes you the best.

This is a very brief description of the DISC personalities. To gain further insight, it is very useful to complete a DISC test for yourself.[131] The personality that you have been given by God is an indicator of the assignment you have received. You are who God says you are, and there is no one who is able to steal this from you. You only need to believe it for yourself.

The Father Wants the Best for You

Sometimes, we think it is God's delight to give us an assignment we hate. We really enjoy the tropical warmth and the beaches, but God will surely send us to the polar regions to teach the Eskimos.

Do we recognize this belief pattern? Our Father is a good Father. He knows the desires of your heart and what is fitting for you. He has made you perfect and loves you greatly. That means that the assignment He has given you is completely tuned in on who *you* are and not the other way around.

For I know the thoughts that I think toward you, says the Lord, thoughts of peace and not of evil, to give you a future and a hope.
Jeremiah 29:11

God's goodness is overwhelming. When you are doing what God has asked you to do, you will come to life. It isn't a punishment or a burden to carry the assignment from your Father. You are created with an inner

---

[131] A short version of a free DISC-test can be found here:
https://discpersonalitytesting.com/free-disc-test/

passion that enables you to overcome any difficulties you encounter. Do the things you naturally like; things that give you energy and that you are passionate about. Take a moment to sit down and write down those things in life that you really care about and what you hate to do. By doing this, you are getter closer to knowing what God's assignment is.

Describe what you really like and what you are passionate about.

This is the essence of the heart of God for you. You will be joyful when you are doing what God has placed in you.

Just a small side note. Don't confuse the passions God has given you with your soulish desires for the things of this world. Be honest to yourself and examine your passions together with the Holy Spirit. He is the one who can show you the best ways. What is truly Him and what are the worldly pleasures? There is great joy in being busy realizing your dreams and your passions.

Then I said, "Behold, I come; In the scroll of the book it is written of me. I delight to do Your will, O my God, and Your law is within my heart."

Psalm 40:7-8

We All Have Received A Special Talent

God has given you all the skills and talents you need in order to fulfill your assignment. If He has called you to write and play the heavenly music on the earth, you are naturally gifted to do so. You'll still have to learn and practice hard to develop your talent and skills. But you can be more successful than someone who is not as gifted as you are.

How often do we see that the contestants in a talent show only have one dream: to show their talent to the whole world, whatever it takes? Write down the things that are easy for you but difficult for others. When people ask for your help, what do they want from you?

Which talents and skills did you receive?

Write down those things where other people are genuinely surprised by you because they see how easy those things are for you to do. These are things that you are equipped to do; that fit you like a glove. You see immediately what needs to be done and you're a natural. Don't walk away from these gifts. Embrace your talents and skills and develop them.

The Prophetic Confirmation

Some have received a prophetic word over their lives. Prophetic words help you to find the right direction in life. Prophecy encourages you, supports you, and corrects you. It is useful to write down every prophetic word you receive.

Which prophetic directions did you receive?

Seek the bottom line in all these encouragements. Most prophecies confirm what you already know on the inside. These prophecies encourage you to reach out further in the realization of your destiny.

The Mood Board

It might help you to create a mood board. In the Netherlands, we have a television show where they help you to redesign your home. In order to create a new living room, the candidates create a mood or vision-board. They use magazines, cutting out any picture that helps them to show their emotional vision, or mood, about their dream room.

The same is true for our desire to fulfill the destiny God has given us. We will really get excited when we walk the walk of God. Sometimes the road can be difficult, but there is something inside us that rejoices because we know that we are on track.

Create a mood board to express your emotions.

Try to express the emotions or mood that you experience when you think about the fulfillment of your dreams. It might help to explore some websites with practical tips on how to create a mood board.[132]

Write Your Scroll

These assignments help you to gain some insight in the content of your scroll. In your own words, write down what you think God has asked you to do. The Father only desires the best for you. The only thing He wants is for you to fulfill your life's calling; that you stand out well. The Father is not a bystander. He isn't a spectator at a game. He is there with you to help you to be successful and He wants to be part of your team. Together with you, He wants to win every game.

When you have completed all the assignments in this chapter, you can start to discover and write down what you experience to be written in your scroll. You know what you like to do and the things you are good at. There will be prophetic confirmations. Realize that your destiny is directly linked to your passion.

Now you might better understand why you have encountered so much resistance in a specific area in your life. When you write these things down, you are also proclaiming and decreeing what your mandate is in the courts of heaven. You are authorized to silence every voice that speaks against your destiny; every voice that hinders you to fulfill God's plan for your life on earth.

Describe the mandate you have been
given by the Father.

Be confident when you decree your destiny before the Father. He testified this over your life the day your scroll was written. Agree with Him and renounce the adversary. In this way, the calling and destiny of your life will be established by the mouth of two or three witnesses.[133] You are allowed to plead on the promises of God for your life. Invoke the assignment God has given. Support these with the prophetic confirmations you

---

[132] http://erinblaskie.com/vision-and-mood-boards/
[133] 2 Corinthians 13:1

have received. Find supporting verses in Scripture. Remind God about the promises He made. Plead, just as Moses did; that it is also in His interest that your destiny on the earth be fulfilled. When you have executed all these assignments, you are capable of writing down the mandate you have received from the Father.

Conclusion

I can almost hear you grumble: "Do I have to do all of this before I can enter the courts of heaven?"

The answer is: "No, you don't have to."

But when you have gained the understanding of the scale of the assignment God has given you, you are much better equipped to present your case in the courts of heaven. So, the answer is also: "Yes, you do. It is for your own benefit."

The mandate you have in the courts of heaven is directly connected with the assignment you have received from God. See the fulfilling of the assignments in the chapter as an investment in your own life. You won't regret a single minute you spend on it because you will finally receive an answer for the most important question in your life: "Why am I on this earth?"

In the next chapter, you will discover why you go to court. You will learn to describe what the injustice is, what has been done to you, and most importantly, how your mandate is supported by Scripture.

13

Describe the Injustice

There can be many reasons to present a case for justice in an earthly court. You could have a conflict with your neighbor, a termination procedure at your work, or even a more serious crime that has been committed against you. You go to court because you are convinced that injustice has been done to you. You want to put the record straight. Perhaps you tried to solve the conflict personally but were unsuccessful. You are convinced that you can persuade the judge to see your point of view. You expect that the judge will vindicate you for everything that has been done to you. You don't go to court because you like to be there. A court case can be an expensive undertaking. In general, the party that loses the lawsuit has to pay for the costs of the trial.

Everyone has the right to present their case before a judge. This is also true in the courts of heaven. We, as citizens of the kingdom of heaven, have obtained the right to present our case before the Heavenly Judge. We see this especially in the life of David, who regularly appealed to God to vindicate him.

For You have maintained my right and my cause; You sat on the throne judging in righteousness.

Psalm 9:4

A Prayer of David. Hear a just cause, O Lord, attend to my cry; Give ear to my prayer which is not from deceitful lips. Let my vindication come from Your presence; let Your eyes look on the things that are upright.

Psalm 17:1-2

Vindicate me, O God, and plead my cause against an ungodly nation; Oh, deliver me from the deceitful and unjust man!

Psalm 43:1

Essentially, you present your case in the courts of heaven to be vindi-cated. Do you realize that the prayers you pray in your inner chamber are heard in the heavenly courtroom? Most of us have been in the courts of heaven more then we realize. It is important that you know precisely what injustice has been done to you. You are not approaching the Judge in order to tell Him that you are sad, or that you are very angry with someone. The Heavenly Judge is not a church counselor who caresses you on the head. He renders a verdict based on the laws of His kingdom. You have to prove, in the court session, that your claim has legal ground. That means that the injustice that has been inflicted upon you must be bibli-cally grounded. This is why you need to prepare yourself.

Single Issue

You need to keep things simple, especially when you are beginning to pray like this. Choose one particular situation in your life; be it at work, church, or a private matter. Then, develop your case based on what is presented here in this chapter. During your first formal court session, you present just one case, *a single issue* so to say, to the Judge.

Don't try to deal with all the injustice that happened in your life in just one court session. Don't engage with the most complicated case. Just begin simply, so that you can learn how the court protocol works. For instance, you might begin with a case like Sven Leeuwestein described in his preface. The moment you start to experience God as the Judge of all the earth and He begins to vindicate you, your faith will grow. You will become more experienced and create a bigger frame of reference.

Who Has Wronged You?

Everyone has experienced a time when they didn't get what they thought they were entitled to---maybe a benefit from the city, a reward, or a pro-motion in your job. You can experience injustice even in church. Leaders can and will make mistakes, or other church members could treat you unjustly. It is not always easy to talk about the things that happened in your life. You may have experienced a great trauma with so much pain that you decided to keep silent about it. The perpetrator might be so in-timidating that you don't dare to tell anyone. But, as long as you are silent, the Heavenly Judge can't render a verdict and vindicate you. It is the same here on earth. The police, the district attorney, and the judge can only act after you have pressed charges.

Describe who wronged you.

But, on the other hand, you could make the mistake of talking to everybody about the alleged crime that has been committed against you. You avoid confronting the one you believe is responsible and begin gossiping about him behind his back.

That is not the way it should be done. First, prepare a list and write down those you hold responsible for the injustice. Think about family members, friends, colleagues at work, or leaders in church. It can also be an organization, a company, or a public authority. The point is, don't start blaming demons or satan. You point out who you think is responsible and let the Heavenly Judge deal with the spiritual powers behind them.

What Happened?

Every time someone hurts you, you experience this as an unlawful act against you. After all, you are being hurt, and that can leave some deep wounds. Still, it is very important to be precise when you describe this injustice. Does it have a biblical foundation? It isn't important if your emotions tell you that something is unlawful; it only matters if the Bible tells you so. When you present your case, the legal grounds can only be found in a violation of the law of the kingdom as described in Scripture, not in your emotional state.

Again, I want to emphasize that your emotions are important, but they aren't decisive when it comes to the issue of guilt.

Describe what happened and support this with facts.

Take time to describe precisely what happened and clarify why you view this as an unlawful act. Be factual and specific and support your case with Scripture. You can always ask someone to help you with this. Tell the court how long these things have been happening. It could be something that happened when you were young or a recent occurrence. It is important to describe the circumstances as precisely as possible.

Did You Seek Peace?

Be aware that we always experience things through the lenses of our own eyes. Your perception and judgment of a situation are, by definition, biased. Most of the time, you don't have a clue about what your opponent experienced unless you have tried to discuss the conflict with him.

Jesus explains the way by which we should solve our conflicts. God asks us first if we are willing to solve the conflict we have with our opponent. You can do this alone, or ask a witness to join you, as one who actually witnessed what happened. When you're unsuccessful in restoring the relationship, you can proceed by presenting your case before the Heavenly Judge. This is what Jesus describes in Matthew.

> *Moreover if your brother sins against you, go and tell him his fault between you and him alone. If he hears you, you have gained your brother. But if he will not hear, take with you one or two more, that 'by the mouth of two or three witnesses every word may be established.' And if he refuses to hear them, tell it to the church. But if he refuses even to hear the church, let him be to you like a heathen and a tax collector.*
>
> *Matthew 18:15-17*

What did you do to restore the relationship?

It is my belief that Jesus is referring to the Beth Din when He speaks about the church. When you aren't able to resolve the conflict by yourself, you can present your case to the Heavenly Judge. That is what you are doing when you enter the mobile court with your witnesses to present your case. But do this only if all other efforts have failed because when you start to plead, the question will be: "What have you done on earth to resolve this conflict? Did you do your best to restore the relationship?"[134]

---

[134] Romans 12:18

It Takes Two to Tango

This old proverb still has its merit. There is seldom a conflict where just one party is to blame. You need to be brutally honest about your part in this conflict. What did *you* do? What negative words did you speak in your anger? Ecclesiastes warns us that we shouldn't curse the king even in our thoughts lest the birds of the air deliver the message.[135]

When you're angry and speak (or even think) evil about your brother, satan can use your testimony as an accusation against your brother. This is the last thing you want because the accusation will not only affect your brother. It will also be used against you.

Describe your role in the conflict.

Be brutally honest with yourself and ask Jesus how He sees the matter. He rules above all parties and will answer you honestly. Sometimes He talks to you directly and sometimes He uses your friends. But, when you don't listen, He will even use your enemies to get the message across. Take the initiative to ask forgiveness from the other person. It doesn't matter if your part in the conflict was small. Don't start to shift the blame entirely to your opponent. That is exactly what Adam and Eve did in paradise. When you do this, you risk being accused in court by your opponent.

Know the Accusation

When you have committed a serious crime, the office of the public prosecutor on earth will take you to court. The district attorney will gather evidence, hear witnesses, and charge you in court. Without a formal accusation, there can be no trial. The indictment has to be grounded on the law of the nation. You can't be charged for something that is not illegal.

Sometimes, you get a sense that someone has taken offense at you. You have no idea what you did wrong, but you are aware of small changes in the relationship. The cordiality and kindness you experienced in the past have changed into a reserved and superficial greeting. You might

---

[135] Ecclesiastes 10:20

experience that people are talking about you, or worse, have accused you in the courts of heaven. What can you do in these circumstances?

You prepare yourself, together with your defense counsel, the best way you can. It is imperative to know and understand the charges and accusations that have been brought to court. One of the most important conditions for a fair trial is the right to know what these are. The district attorney has to tell you what the charges are and what the evidence is. There can even be a mistrial when the district attorney withholds evidence.

What are the charges brought against you?

This is also true in the courts of heaven. You have the right to know what charges are being brought against you. This doesn't only apply to the accusations that satan has brought into court; it also applies to the accusations that are brought in by other human beings.

This is what Jesus warns us about in the sermon on the mount. When you are going to court and your adversary is accusing you, he urges you to agree with them quickly. If you don't do this, you risk being condemned yourself.[136]

This is why it is so important to be transparent and honest in your research into the reasons behind the conflict. Ask the Holy Spirit what charges have been brought against you. Then be honest and acknowledge your part.

What Are the Lies of The Enemy?

One of the legal tactics the enemy uses is to put all the blame at your doorstep. He does this by gossiping and spreading lies about you. The result can be that you constantly think negative about yourself. You take the blame for things you didn't do, or, conversely, you blame everybody else for the trouble you are in.

One of the most difficult things to do is to set the record straight concerning the inner vows and thoughts you have, unless you make them

---

[136] Matthew 5:25-26

public. As long as you are silent about the accusations that you hear in your mind, the enemy can control your life. The moment you come clean and reveal those inner thoughts, the truth can shine upon it. This is why it is important to do this process with someone else. You have received the right to silence every tongue that has turned against you in court.[137] Do not let the lies of the enemy paralyze you any longer.

Let me give an example. After Jesus was born, everybody in Israel was aware that something was happening. There were signs at His birth— Magi who came from the east, angels that appeared to the shepherds, and so on. These events brought hope into the hearts of the people of Israel. But not everybody was pleased with the arrival of this Messiah.

What lies are accusing you?

It was satan that caused Herod to kill all the boys in Bethlehem aged two years and younger. In this manner, he tried to destroy the destiny of Jesus by killing Him and countless others. His plan utterly failed because the angels of God warned Joseph in time. But can you imagine the burden Jesus had to carry?

Satan didn't succeed in killing Jesus, but I can imagine that he put the blame for the murder of thousands of innocent boys on Jesus: "Because you were born, they had to die!"

This is what satan also does with us. He only wants one thing: to hinder us by any means necessary in order to destroy our destinies. When he can't touch us, he tries to put pressure on us by telling us all kinds of lies, in order to completely undermine us.

Proclaim God's Righteousness

After you have described the injustice afflicted upon you, you begin to balance this evil with the promises God made in His Word. What does the Bible say about healing, deliverance, providence, and restoration? God watches over the widow and orphans--those who have to walk alone in life. Use these promises in the Word of God to support your plea.

---

[137] Isaiah 54:17

Support your plea with Scripture

You start with the presentation of your case by writing down the answers to the questions and the assignment mentioned in this chapter. Support these as much as possible with verses from Scripture. You can find a lot of them in the Psalms and Proverbs of Solomon. But, also take a look at the book of Job. You can read how he presents his case before the Almighty One. Use your own words to present your complaints or demands. Be specific, be clear, be transparent, and be loving.

Conclusion

The assignments in this chapter might be the most difficult of the entire book. It is here that you get to the root of the injustice that has been afflicted upon you. It is so important to put into words your version of what happened. Take your time to do that. The first time is always exciting and perhaps difficult. After all, you don't yet have a frame of reference for this new undertaking.

Perhaps you are reading this book because some injustice has been afflicted on you, or you are merely interested in the subject, but as you read, the Holy Spirit is shedding His Light on some of the things that have happened to you. Chances are, it has been going on for a while. The pain is intense, the frustration is great, and the emotions can barely be controlled.

But the end of your sorrow is near. There is a Judge in heaven waiting eagerly for you. He happens to be your Father and Friend. Your brother, Jesus, is your Advocate that stands beside you. When you have followed this procedure at length, you will see that it will become easier and quicker.

Finally, in the next chapter, you will enter the courtroom and present your case to the Heavenly Judge.

14

Come, Let Us Adjudge Together

Every court session is structured in a consistent manner. When the Judge is seated, the court is in session. Everyone that plays a part in the court session needs to confirm their identities, such as the lawyer, advisors, witnesses, and expert witnesses. The case is presented, witnesses are heard, and in the end, the Judge renders a verdict.

To my knowledge, the courts of heaven do not operate with a jury system. In the heavenly court system, the judge hears all the pleas, makes the decision, renders a verdict, and determines the sentence. You approach the Heavenly Judge in faith; He is also your Father and Friend. Because He is in an official capacity, you address Him as "Heavenly Judge." This is the way to show respect to the office and role the Almighty One holds at that moment.

Don't forget that entering the courtroom and perceiving what is happening there is all done by taking a step in faith. It will help you to picture the courtroom. The Judge sits right before you. Jesus Christ is your Advocate and stands next to you. On the other side of the room sits your adversary. There are benches where the witnesses are seated and there is a scribe who records everything that happens. There is also a public gallery where the others are watching what is happening. The invitation has been sent and heaven is eagerly waiting. When will the saints of the Most High reply to His invitation?

"Come now, and let us reason together," says the Lord, "Though your sins are like scarlet, they shall be as white as snow; though they are red like crimson, they shall be as wool."

Isaiah 1:18

In the Dutch translation, we read: *Come now, let us go into court and settle the matter.* In Hebrew, it says: *Let us adjudge together.* It is as if the Father invites us to present our case—our life—in His Court. He promises us He will cleanse and purify us.

Preparation of the Court Session

You are guided step-by-step in this chapter through the different stages of the trial. In order to assist you, all the prayers are written down so you can say them out loud. When you've done your homework, all the assignments in the previous chapters are finished. That includes investigation of the content in your scroll, so that you will know which mandate you have in order to plead properly. You have also searched out what kind of injustice has been done to you and which role you played in the conflict. You have chosen a single issue, not all the injustices of your whole life.

You have blessed your enemies and have asked forgiveness for the things you did in the conflict. During this session, everything mentioned there will be dealt with. Take your time to enter the rest of your Father. Make arrangements so that you're not disturbed. (Turn off your phone!). It will benefit you greatly when you do this with someone else, especially when you do this for the first time. Together, you are much more capable to perceive what is going on in the heavenly courtroom. Perhaps you could take communion together before you start.

When you prepare your court session, it is good to start thanking God in prayer. Emphasize that you are coming into His court in order to lift up His name. It is your desire that His will shall be done on earth as it is in heaven. Tell Him that you don't seek your own honor, but the honor of the Almighty One, of His Son Jesus Christ, and of the Holy Spirit. Confess that righteousness and justice are the foundation of His throne.

Opening the Court Session

In this part, you recognize the authority of the Judge overall and demand that everyone present in this court session does the same. It is very important that you only speak to the Heavenly Judge. Everything that is being said is spoken to Him. Just as in a court on the earth, the Judge will open the session.

Heavenly Judge, I appear before You in the name of the Lord Jesus Christ and in the blood of the Lamb. I acknowledge that You have all the power in heaven, on and under the earth. You have all dominion. I acknowledge that this court is authorized to render a verdict in the case that is presented before You. Heavenly Judge, I ask You to open this court session.

I also request that everybody who is involved in this lawsuit is   present in this courtroom. I ask that all books that have relevance are opened. We subject ourselves and everyone present under the power of the blood of the Lamb.

I declare that I will tell the truth and nothing but the truth, I will not withhold anything during this session. I declare that I have done all things reasonable in order to restore the relationship with my opponent, in order to discuss the injustice I have experienced.

Confession of Faith

Just as in an earthly court, it is important that your identity is confirmed. This is the reason you profess your faith; so that everybody in the heavenly court knows who you are and what your position is. You also take your responsibility for the iniquities and sins of your ancestors. You act like a priest on their behalf. This prevents satan from using the sins of your ancestors as a basis to say you are inadmissible. When you declare this confession of faith, you also deal with any oaths or covenants that have been taken or sealed by your ancestors.

Heavenly Judge, I .... (full name) confess that Jesus Christ of Nazareth has come in the flesh. I confess that He died on the cross and that He shed His blood for the salvation of my soul. I confess that Your Son is risen from the dead and is now standing at my side to plead on my behalf. I confess that this Jesus is the Christ and my Lord.

> Heavenly Judge, I ask You to judge me according to Your perfect Law,
> the Torah. I confess that I am responsible for every transgression, sin,
> and iniquity that I have performed. I also confess this on behalf of the
> transgressions, sins, and iniquities of my ancestors. I take responsibil-
> ity for their actions and the consequences thereof.
>
> I position myself in Christ. I have died on the cross with Him. I ask You
> to place any punishment for my sins on Christ there on the cross. I ask
> forgiveness for all these transgressions, sins, and iniquities, based on
> the sacrifice of Jesus Christ on the cross and the blood of the Lamb
> that has been shed for me. I ask that You judge everyone that is in-
> volved in this court session in the same way.

Stating Your Mandate

When you have prepared your court case, you have determined the mandate you have to present this specific case to the Heavenly Judge. You are
presenting your case because there is a personal injustice, or you are
mandated by someone else to plead their case. You establish this mandate before you begin. The person who is asking you to present them in
the heavenly court must, of course, be authorized to do so.

> Heavenly Judge, based on the destiny You have given me, or based on
> the power that has been given to me, I declare that I am mandated to
> present this case before You and to plead   accordingly.
> Heavenly Judge, You have given me the assignment to fulfill this des-
> tiny on the earth. I declare that satan is obstructing me to prevent me
> from realizing this destiny according to Your will.

Forgive and Be Forgiven

During your preparation, you have described the injustice that has been
done to you. This is the moment to take some time and ask for forgiveness
for the role you played in the conflict. You forgive those who have hurt
you. You speak a blessing over their lives. When an organization has

wronged you, forgive those who are responsible. Don't let a bitter root grow in your heart. Revoke the negative word you have spoken in anger or frustration.

> I forgive those who have hurt me in any way. I choose not to be bitter but to do everything I can to restore the relationship. I revoke any negative words I have spoken about my opponent in anger or frustration. I ask that these words are blotted out by the blood of the Lamb, from any book where they might have been written down.
>
> I ask forgiveness for every role I played in this conflict I have with my opponent. (Be specific in what way you were responsible.)
>
> I ask forgiveness of any person who has been harmed in any way. I ask for restoration of the damages these people have   experienced that are the result of the things I have done or said.

The Plea

Based on the injustice that has been inflicted upon you, you are mandated to press charges before the Heavenly Judge against your opponent. You are allowed to ask for compensation for any loss or damages that you have suffered. Ask for the restoration of your destiny and of anything that has illegally been robbed from you. The Heavenly Judge will make the final decision about the legitimacy of your demands.

During this plea, you explain what injustice has been done to you. You name the facts, present the evidence, and tell the Judge what kind of loss you have experienced. Then you explain who you think is responsible for this. Don't forget that you only address the Heavenly Judge; you do not speak to the other parties present.

Try to be as specific as possible, but avoid long stories. Let the Word of God be the basis of your plea, not only to describe the injustice, but also to support your demands for compensation. Use the notes you have written when you fulfilled the assignments in the previous chapters.

Heavenly Judge, I press charges against .... (name the persons/organizations) that have wronged me. I ask that You judge them just as You have judged me. Heavenly Judge, I ask, according to my confession, that You deny my opponents any legal rights to hinder me any longer in the realization of my destiny.

Heavenly Judge, I willingly part from any advantage that I, or my ancestors, have received as a result of any covenant made with the powers of darkness. I ask that any covenant made between the powers of darkness and my bloodline be dissolved. I renounce any claim satan has on my life and on my bloodline.

Heavenly Judge, I ask that divorce papers be drafted, and I ask You to sign them so that they might be enforced. I demand that any seal that any enemy or opponent has placed on my scroll be broken so that my scroll can be opened and read.

Heavenly Judge, I am asking for proper compensation for any damage or loss that these injustices have caused in my life.

When you ask for compensation, be specific. For instance, you could mention that your opponents keep the promises that were made, such as deliverance, healing, or restoration. Be careful that your demands don't come from your fleshly desires but are aligned with the will of God for your life. The will of God isn't hard to understand. He desires what is good, acceptable, and perfect for your life.[138] Name the boundary stones that you want to place, in order to decrease the power of satan over your life.[139]

Finish your prayer by blessing the persons that stand against you in this case. Proclaim that they also will realize their God-given destiny. Ask that everything that belongs to them is cleansed by the blood of the Lamb.

---

[138] Romans 12:2;
[139] Page 50

Witness Statements and Evidence

Just like in an earthly court, every party gets the opportunity to speak. Your opponent is allowed to present their statement in the courtroom, order to also present their point of view. Ask your friends who are with you in this prayer to write down what they experience or perceive.

> Heavenly Judge, I ask You to allow my opponent to present their case. I also ask that You give the witnesses the opportunity to testify. I ask that any hidden or public accusations against me be brought into the courtroom. I also ask that any evidence is presented.
>
> Heavenly Judge, I ask You to show me which accusations against me have a legal right. I take responsibility for anything that I am accused of and confess this in Your presence.

Take some time to do this.

> I call upon the blood of the Lamb in order to receive forgiveness for all my transgressions.
>
> Heavenly Judge, I ask You, according to the blood of the Lamb, to destroy all evidence presented against me. I decree and   declare that Jesus Christ has conquered all my enemies.   Because I am crucified with Christ, I, too, have conquered all my enemies.

The Verdict of the Judge

After you have pressed charges against your opponent before the Judge, you ask Him to render a verdict and to meet your demands. Ask those who pray with you to tell you what they perceive in the courtroom. After you have received the written verdict of the Heavenly Judge, you need to write down this verdict. You can also record any prophetic revelation that your friends receive, but it is important to write down the verdict of the Judge.

> Heavenly Judge, I ask You to render a verdict on my behalf concerning the charges I have presented before You. I ask You to meet my demands. I also ask You to hand over the verdict and the divorce papers that go with it. Thank You, Heavenly Judge, that You judge in righteousness. I believe that I have received Your verdict together with the divorce papers.

Take your time to write down any impressions you and your friends receive. Let everyone who is praying with you tell you what they perceive in the courtroom. This is an important step because the verdict of the Judge is binding for all parties. Ask the Holy Spirit if He wants to help you to hear and understand the voice of the Judge.

Conclusion of the Court Session

After you have received the verdict of the Heavenly Judge, the time has come to close this court session. You, therefore, ask the Heavenly Judge to close this session and to bless everyone who is present in this session.

> Heavenly Judge, I thank You for your goodness and mercy. I thank You that You have judged in righteousness according to Your Word. I praise Your name and honor You. Lord Jesus, You are worthy to receive all power, riches, wisdom, strength, honor, glory, and thanksgiving, forever and ever. Holy Spirit, I thank You that You have assisted me in this court case with all wisdom and counsel.
>
> Heavenly Judge, I ask You for the leadership of the Holy Spirit and the Seven Spirits of God, in order to be able to execute the written verdict. I ask permission to deploy the Hosts of heaven on my behalf, to execute the written judgment.
>
> Heavenly Judge, I ask You to close this court session. I declare that I have performed this session under the authority of Jesus Christ and that I am protected by Him after this session.

15

Execute the Written Judgment

Congratulations! You have just finished your first heavenly court case. Be aware that your Father in heaven has longed for this moment very much. His heart is full of goodness and peace for you. It is full of desire and passion to walk with you and to see you realize your dreams.

You are in the possession of a written verdict from your first court case. Make it last! The whole process you just went through is a great challenge for your faith. As you appear in the heavenly courts more often, you will perceive more of what is going on there because you are developing a frame of reference. A new beginning can be difficult, so I advise you to read more about the way the courts of heaven function.

As I said before, it is important to develop your perception of the spirit realm. Try to practice your spiritual senses. Follow a training program or sign up for the NEST. This is a three-year training program where you learn how to engage the spiritual dimensions as a mature son or daughter of God.[140] You can also enroll as a student at Aactev8 Academy. You will learn what the Father has had in store for us since the foundation of the world.[141]

What do you do after the court is closed? First of all, thank the Heavenly Judge for giving you justice and vindicating you. You are convinced that He only wants the best for you. This is what Jesus promised us the Father would do.[142]

It is God's desire to bless you with the best heaven has to offer. It is His wish that you fulfill your destiny, and He is longing to help you with that.

I realize that it can be difficult to interpret the verdict of the Heavenly Judge properly. It can be just as hard as to understand what God is saying

---

[140] For more information see http://www.thefoundationnest.com
[141] For more information see http://www.aactev8.com/start
[142] Matthew 7:11

to you personally. Though you may be capable of speaking an encourage-ment over someone else, when you are in the middle of it, the intensity of your emotions and thoughts can make it difficult to hear the voice of God properly. There can be a lot of questions going on in your mind. Did I hear this correctly? Are these my own desires? Did I really get what I asked for?

These are all legitimate questions. For this reason, I want to give you something to go on. After you have received the verdict of the Judge, it is imperative to write it down as soon as possible. That why it is so im-portant that you are supported by some friends, especially when it is the first time you do this. Your friends might better understand and perceive what the Father is really saying, and what are your own thoughts and emotions.

Writing the judgment down is important; this is a biblical principle. Every decision that God makes when He sits on His throne is called a Royal Decree. We have the same here in the Netherlands. Our parliament can make a law, but only after the king has signed it does it becomes offi-cial. The law has no legal force until it is signed.

This is why it is so important to know what is written in the council decision. The decisions of the Council of the Lord are supposed to be en-forced on the earth, but that won't happen by itself.

Let me give a biblical example. We all know the content of the Lord's prayer. It is the prayer that Jesus taught His disciples when they asked Him how they should pray. (For this reason alone, it should be called *The Disciples' Prayer*).

> *So He said to them, "When you pray, say: Our Father in heaven, hal-lowed be Your name. Your kingdom come. Your will be done on earth as it is in heaven."*
>
> *Luke 11:2*

Jesus tells them that the will of God is done in heaven, but that it is the task of the disciples to see that the will of God is done on the earth. The will of God is recorded in a Royal Decree and signed by Him. The Bible calls this the counsel of the Lord. However, this counsel must arrive on the earth to enforce its legal power. Please read carefully; there is a dif-ference between the *counsel* of the Lord, which is a Royal Decree, and the *council* of the Lord. This is the executive Beth Din over the whole creation.

The Vision of Daniel

We read in Daniel 10 that a word is revealed to Daniel pertaining to a large battle. Daniel understood this word and received an understanding about his vision. He decided to fast for three weeks for the salvation of his people. At the end of the three weeks, an angel arrived with a message from the throne for him. This angel was sent out the moment Daniel started pleading for his nation, but on his way to the earth, the angel was greatly hindered. As long as the message hadn't landed on the earth, the will of God could not be done here. At the end of this story, we see that this angel had a book for Daniel.

> But I will tell you what is noted in the Scripture of Truth. (No one upholds me against these, except Michael your prince).
>
> *Daniel 10:21*

Daniel gains a better understanding of the future of his nation. But he also receives the order to seal the words he just heard. How does he do this? He does this by sealing the book until the end times. As long as the book is sealed, the content thereof is a mystery.

In the book of Revelation, we see the same principle. John was in the heavens and saw a scroll that was sealed with seven seals. There was a loud voice that asked if anyone was worthy to break the seals of this scroll. John was crying because there was no one in heaven, on the earth, or under the earth, who was worthy to open the scroll and read or see the content thereof.

Have you ever wondered why John had to cry so much? The answer might surprise you. As long as the scroll is closed, nobody is able to read its content. That means that any counsel of the Lord and any destiny that is written in this scroll can't be decreed on the earth. This is why it is so important that the scrolls are opened and decreed because then the content of the scroll has the power of law. As long as somebody can't read the counsel of the Heavenly Judge, demons aren't hindered in their wicked ways on earth.

The enemy furiously resists the disclosure of the counsels of the Lord because every counsel that is being enforced on the earth is a direct act of war on his domain. Every child of God that is vindicated by the Heavenly Judge will suffer the enemy a crushing defeat. When God's children are fulfilling their destinies, heaven rejoices because this is how God's works are made visible on the earth.

Now you have received a verdict that is signed by the Heavenly Judge. This counsel of the Lord contains all decisions concerning the demands you have made in the court case. You should have received an answer to any demand you had. Now it is up to you to bring this will of God to the earth and execute the content.

Landing the Scroll

The prophet Zechariah had a vision where he saw a flying scroll. Yes, you read that correctly: a *flying* scroll. The Lord explained to Zechariah that this scroll contained a decree from the throne and a verdict over the unrighteous. It was a decision made in heaven about the thieves and perjurers on the earth.

What we can learn from this vision is that the counsels of the Lord come to the earth as a flying scroll. This scroll only receives the power of law when there is someone on the earth who knows what is written in it and subsequently decrees it. That is the purpose of all prophetic books in the Bible; to describe and decree the visions the prophet received in heaven. This is the only way to give those counsels of the Lord power of law.

> Surely the Lord God does nothing, unless He reveals His secret to His servants the prophets. A lion has roared! Who will not fear? The Lord God has spoken! Who can but prophesy?
>
> *Amos 3:7-8*

Let me give a personal example. In order to become an officer in the Royal Dutch Navy, a Royal Decree has to be signed by the king. The same is true for every promotion you receive in the navy. When you have finished your training as an officer, the whole class can be sworn in at the same fixed date. But though everyone knows that you are promoted on that date, you still must wait until the king has signed the Royal Decree.

As long as this Royal Decree isn't signed by the king, you are not allowed to wear the insignia of your rank. Only after the Royal Decree has been handed over to you by your commanding officer, are you allowed to wear the insignias. It is then you gain the authority, the power and the jurisdiction that belongs to your rank.

The same is true for the verdict of the heavenly court. Even if everybody knows what is written in it, you can only act upon it after you have proclaimed the written verdict on the earth. This happened to Zechariah and Daniel. The decrees from the Heavenly Judge were only activated after someone proclaimed them on the earth.

Our Assignment

Now what to do with all this information? I hope you understand why it is important to write down the verdict from heaven. You have a counsel of the Lord in your hands. This decree has the power of law when you use your mandate to reveal its content. There is no power in darkness that is able to stop you from doing this when you walk in authority. Perhaps this is what Jesus meant when He said:

> I speak what I have seen with My Father, and you do what you have seen with your father."
>
> John 8:38

The reason we go to the heavenly court is because someone has wronged us. We ask God to vindicate us and give us justice. Now that we have received the written verdict, we have obtained what we asked for. But it is not the task of the Judge to enforce the verdict. The same is true on earth.

Let me give an example. In my neighborhood, there was a large building that was empty. It didn't take long for some squatters to occupy the building. These squatters caused a lot of trouble and started doing criminal activities.

Of course, the owner of this building wasn't pleased. Besides the fact that he couldn't sell his property, the squatters were also causing a lot of damage. But in the Netherlands, an owner is not allowed to throw out intruders, even if the squatters gained access to his building illegally. The police couldn't help the owner either because they didn't know if the owner had made an agreement with the squatters and just wanted them out.

So, the owner had to go to court first, before he could remove the intruders from his building. He had to obtain a verdict about the illegitimacy of the invasion of his property. He had to prove in court that the squatters were occupying his property illegally and that no agreement had been made with them. He also had to demand the evacuation of his premises and that the squatters pay for the damage they caused. In this particular case, the judge ruled in his favor. The judge rendered a verdict which stated that the occupation was illegal and ordered the evacuation of the squatters. This verdict was handed to the owner.

The owner was very pleased and went to his property. He stood in front of the building with the written verdict waving in his hand. The squatters were docile and began leaving the building after they had cleaned up their mess...no, not really. The squatters didn't budge, and so the police arrived on the scene. The squatters didn't care about the verdict of the judge because they didn't recognize his authority.

Luckily for the owner, we have an executive legal power---the police force. The SWAT team went in the building and cleared it within 30 minutes. The evacuation was a fact. The resistance of the squatters was broken because there was an executive legal power that was mandated to use force in order to remove the squatters from the building.

The Hosts of Heaven

We all recognize the road the owner had to take in order to get his property back. Somebody wronged you, you go to court and receive a verdict from the Judge in heaven.

But then what? Sometimes things don't really change. When this happens, you can ask the executive powers of heaven to assist you. This is the army of the Lord; the hosts of heaven. They will happily help you in the execution of the verdict. We see this also in the vision of the flying scroll.

"I will send out the curse," says the Lord of Hosts.

Zechariah 5:4

The Bible tells us here that it is the Lord of Hosts who has rendered the verdict. This means that the hosts of heaven are involved with the execution of the verdict. You can appeal to this host of heavenly beings. The army of the Lord is sent out to help us to subdue the enemy on the earth. I will explain this with a verse from Hebrews.

But to which of the angels has he ever said: "Sit at My right hand, till
I make Your enemies Your footstool"? Are they not all ministering
spirits sent forth to minister for those who will inherit salvation?
Hebrews 1:13-14

None of the angels ever heard that they were allowed to sit at the right
hand of the Almighty One. These words were spoken to the Son and contain a promise and an assignment. The promise is that all the enemies of
the Messiah are to be made a footstool for His feet. We already have seen
that the earth is the footstool of His feet. So, the location where His enemies are subdued is the earth. The assignment to fulfill this promise is
given to us, the church, but the hosts of heaven fulfill an important role.
They are sent from the throne to the earth to assist the saints in the execution of their assignment.

The armies of the Lord are here to help us to execute the counsels of
the Lord on the earth. But they are waiting for us. We have the initiative;
we, the sons of the living God. We are the ones who must receive these
counsels of the Lord and proclaim them on the earth.

This is what a bailiff does. He takes the verdict of a judge and comes
with a warrant. On this warrant is written in capitals: IN THE NAME OF
THE KING. Then we read the verdict of the judge that must be executed.

We read in Psalm 149 that God has given us the right to execute His
written judgments. This is what gives us our glory: that His enemies are
made a footstool for His feet, through our doing.

To execute vengeance on the nations, and punishments on the peo-
ples; to bind their kings with chains, and their nobles with fetters of
iron; to execute on them the written judgment— this honor have all
His saints. Praise the Lord!
Psalm 149:7-9

God has vested us with authority and mandated us to proclaim the counsels of the Lord on the earth. The moment we cry out: *"IN THE NAME OF*
THE KING!" every power in darkness shivers. Not just because of the
court order, but also because of the mighty hosts of heaven that accom-
pany us. They will enforce the correct execution of the counsels of the
Lord on the earth.

This is the way the authority of the kingdom of heaven operates. This is what the centurion knew when he came to Jesus on behalf of his sick servant. He was someone in authority and he knew very well that Jesus functioned in the same way he did.

> "Lord, my servant is lying at home paralyzed, dreadfully tormented." And Jesus said to him, "I will come and heal him." The centurion answered and said, "Lord, I am not worthy that You should come under my roof. But only speak a word, and my servant will be healed.
> For I also am a man under authority, having soldiers under me. And I say to this one, 'Go,' and he goes; and to another, 'Come,' and he comes; and to my servant, 'Do this,' and he does it." When Jesus heard it, he marveled, and said to those who followed, "Assuredly, I say to you, I have not found such great faith, not even in Israel!"
>
> *Matthew 8:6-10*

The moment you receive the written judgment of the Judge, the only thing you have to do is to proclaim this counsel of the Lord on the earth. Because you have presented your case in the courts of heaven, you are authorized to enforce righteousness and justice on the earth.

You do this by decreeing the written judgment. You can't own this authority by your faith or by your righteousness; it is rooted in the kingship of our God. His kingdom is an eternal kingdom. The scepter of God, the symbol of his authority and power, is a scepter of righteousness.

> But to the Son He says: "Your throne, O God, is forever and ever; a scepter of righteousness is the scepter of Your kingdom. You have loved righteousness and hated lawlessness; therefore God, Your God, has anointed You With the oil of gladness more than Your companions."
>
> *Hebrews 1:8-9*

Know that God has called us to rule with Him as kings. He gives us the authority to sit on the judge's bench in order to judge and render a verdict. Then we are able to discern with our own eyes between good and evil.

Conclusion

Let us take the position that Christ has prepared for us with great boldness. Let us come into action and present our case before the Heavenly Judge, in order to deal with the injustice that has been done to us.

Creation is suppressed by the terror of the enemy. It is waiting for its redemption. It is waiting on the revelation of the sons and daughters of God. It is up to us, the sons and daughters of the Living God, to execute the will of God on the earth, to plead for righteousness, and to decree the judgments of our God.

Therefore, take the judgment of the Heavenly Judge. Decree and declare the counsel of the throne and say to your enemies:

"IN THE NAME OF THE KING!"

Epilogue

For months now, the heavenly streets have been buzzing with excitement. Everybody is talking about it. Will the saints of the Most High God finally make their appearance before Him? The angels rush to the great hall. There is so much to be done in these last moments. Some are preparing the banquet. There, the sons of the Most High God will dine with Him after the ceremony.

The anticipation is palpable in the great stately courtroom. Everything is prepared. Thrones are made ready; the witnesses take their places. Representatives of all tongues, tribes, and nations are seated in the gallery in their beautiful white linen. The scribes have been working furiously in order to prepare all the books. It could be that the dark prince, the accuser of the brethren, will enter yet another false statement.

The waiting is almost over. Everybody is so happy that the desire of the Father will finally be fulfilled. Even the Son of the Most High is very excited. This is the moment the whole of creation has been waiting for: All the enemies of the Messiah are made a footstool under His feet.

The dark prince has been in panic mode for weeks now, knowing his end has arrived. He has opened his bag of tricks, as expected. Religious spirits have worked on overtime in order to confuse the church in these last moments. Because of their activities the hashtag #showmeinscripture? is on top of the Twitter charts. Lying spirits have whispered all kinds of stories in the ears of the saints: "*You only get into heaven when you die. You don't have any authority on the earth. You are not mandated to judge the angels. You will never fulfill your destiny. The rapture of the church will make an end to your suffering. The earth will be a terrible place before His return.*"

More lies have been spread, and every news outlet has become a fake news site. Social media is running wild with all these lies and accusations.

But it is the Spirit of the Most High that triumphs in the end. He is the One who will convince the children of God that they are entitled to plead before the throne of God. The time for restoration is now; the time the saints will receive the kingdom is now. The ancient promises are finally being realized. The books that have been sealed by Daniel and John are finally read by the saints on the earth. Waves of happiness and joy fill the earth. The saints know that the door to heaven has been opened.

Suddenly, shofars are blown. Everybody rises. The door of the stately room slowly opens. Lights come from the earth and begin to enter heaven. First a few, but more soon follow. A complete sea of light is entering the great council of the Lord in a steady stream. Finally, the sons and daughters of the Lord arrive.

One after another is escorted inside by the archangels, and they take their positions. The Son of the Most High has the biggest smile on His face you have ever seen. He is delirious with joy.

Then, when everybody has arrived, the doors close. Everyone grows quiet and they rise in honor of the entrance of the Supreme Judge. Behind the great white throne, another door opens. An overwhelming clear light, with more colors than the rainbow ever had, dances into the hall. Beneath the throne, a sea of fire starts to move. A herald stamps his rod on the floor and proclaims with a loud voice: *"The Ancient of Days, The Judge over all the Earth, The King of the whole creation."*

All hail the King of Glory. Some weep for joy. There comes the Ancient of Days, shining like the sun; entering the great hall. He sits on His glorious throne and everyone is seated. It takes some time before everyone calms down, but He is enjoying every moment of it.

The court is now in session. One after another, the saints give their statements. Full of fire, they proclaim the victories they've achieved on the enemies of the Most High God. They ask the Judge to vindicate them and that their blood be revenged.

The dark prince becomes more and more anxious. You can see the fear in his eyes. His domain is crumbling. His power is broken. One by one, his dark servants are ordered to appear in the majestic courtroom.

"Kneel!" the saints of God order them in unison. Their voices are like the thunder, like the sound of a trumpet thundering through creation. There, before the throne of the Lamb, all servants of the dark prince bow their knees and confess that Jesus Christ is Lord. They acknowledge that all power, all honor, and all strength belong to Him!

The earth rejoices. Freedom at last! The heavens are stirred. The stars are dancing for joy. This hasn't happened since the day God said: *"Let there be Light!"*

Finally, the sons and daughters of God are revealed in their glory. The kingdom and the dominion have been given to the saints of the Most High.

Creation awakens from a coma. City after city, district after district, nation after nation, and every continent is delivered from the smothering domination of the dark prince.

This is only the beginning. The kingdom of the Most High shall be given to all His saints. They receive the dominion that Adam lost in the garden. These are the wages they have anticipated for so long. The whole universe shall be restored.

More judgments are made. In the end, the dark prince stands completely alone before the throne of the Ancient of Days. The river of fire has engulfed him. The wheels beneath the throne are burning intensively.

Then he is judged, together with death and hades. The dominion of the evil one is finally broken; humanity and creation celebrate their deliverance. The dark prince, death, and hades are led to the abyss. Everyone is full of joy as hell finally receives its eternal punishment.

The Ancient of Days closes the court session. Everyone is cheering so loudly that even the black holes in the universe comes to life and starts shining. The banquet begins. The time has come for the wedding feast of the Lamb.

But the court shall be seated,
And they shall take away his dominion,

To consume and destroy it forever.
Then the kingdom and dominion,

And the greatness of the kingdoms under the whole heaven,
Shall be given to the people, the saints of the Most High.

His kingdom is an everlasting kingdom,
And all dominions shall serve and obey Him.

Daniel 7:26-27

Announcement of the Messiah's Reign

A Psalm of David.

The Lord said to my Lord,
"Sit at My right hand,
Till I make Your enemies Your footstool."

The Lord shall send the rod of Your strength out of Zion.
Rule in the midst of Your enemies!

Your people shall be volunteers
In the day of Your power;

In the beauties of holiness, from the womb of the morning,
You have the dew of Your youth.

The Lord has sworn
And will not relent,

"You are a priest forever
According to the order of Melchizedek."

The Lord is at Your right hand;
He shall execute kings in the day of his wrath.

He shall judge among the nations,
He shall fill the places with dead bodies,
He shall execute the heads of many countries.

He shall drink of the brook by the wayside;
Therefore He shall lift up the head.

Psalm 110

Acknowledgments

First of all, I want to thank the Triune God, for their support, their understanding, and supernatural power they gave me in writing this book.

My Father, You are also *my* Judge. It is a privilege to stand before You. Jesus Christ, You are my Advocate, my wonderful Counselor: You plead for me in the courtroom. Holy Spirit, You are the Helper at my side. It is a privilege to have You as my Mentor.

I thank the seven Spirits of God. They are my Teachers. They support and help me. You speak to me: *"This is the way: walk before me."*

I thank Noortje, my loving wife, for the inspiration, the freedom, the love, and support you give me in my life. *You are the sunshine of my life.*

I thank Dick and Arleen for years of friendship. It is a privilege to know you.

I thank Arjan, Meindert and Marie-Thérèse, and Peter for their piercing questions. You have made this book sharper than a two-edged sword.

I thank Sven for the beautiful preface, where you testify that the courts of heaven will justify you.

I thank John and Beverley for their recommendations. Some encounters were destined from heaven. This is one of them.

I thank Roos, Jim and Diane for the professional support in editing this book. What you bring to the table is invaluable.

I thank Anneke. You have gone meticulously through the manuscript to enhance the quality. Your precision is unprecedented.

I thank my friends for the years they kept believing in me. Without your prayers and prophetic encouragements, this book wouldn't exist.

I thank Ian Clayton and Dr. Adonijah Ogbonnaya for the way you prepared for us. Your selfless efforts will mature many sons.

Recommended Literature

Manual courts of heaven for beginners
Ronald Montijn
Publishing House Seferim

This workbook is a supplement for the paperback edition. It will help you to prepare your court case and present your case to the heavenly Judge.

There is ample space to work on the assingments mentioned in the paperback edition.

You can make additional notes and have permission to make copies of the workbook once you have purchased one copy of it.

There is an index of the Scriptural reference so you are able to study this subject in depth.

Realms of the kingdom Volume 1

Ian Clayton

Seraph Creative

Realms of the Kingdom will equip believers with the reality of what it means to be 'in the spirit' and in the realms of God, enabling them to know and experience who the person of God really is. The book will be a valuable resource enabling you to actively participate with and know your Father God, not just doing things for Him.

This book is for those who want to see the reality of the supernatural realms of Heaven and the return of the sons of the Kingdom to their rightful place as heirs.

This second edition of Volume 1 will lead you on a journey through Ian's experiences in heavenly realms and includes spiritual steps and prayer activations enabling you to understand, experience and enter these realms for yourself.

This book includes chapters on: Eden, The River, The Dark Cloud, The Courtroom of God, The Seven Spirits of God, Spirit/Soul Gateways, Spiritual Crowns and Using the Word as a Doorway.

Ian Clayton is the founder of Son of Thunder Ministries. He speaks globally, training and equipping believers to personally experience the realms of Heaven.

Ian Clayton is one of the fathers of current heavenly realms understanding. His original, ground-breaking teaching and practical insights, gained over more than 25 years, have changed the way our generation experience accessing the realms of Heaven that Jesus has opened to us.

HASHAMAYIM 1A
השמים
ANGELS, HEAVENLY STRUCTURES & THE SONS OF GOD

DR. ADONIJAH OGBONNAYA

HaShamayim 1A: Angels, Heavenly Structures and the Sons of God

Dr. A. Ogbonnaya

Aactev8 International

If a believer is born from above, is it not logical then that the believer should return there as often as he or she desires or is able? If the believer is seated in the heavenlies, does it not call forth a need to understand what the heavens looks like?

I began very early in my journey to ask for understanding of how heaven is structured and also to seek for a language on how to narrate my experiences. These experiences are the results of my travel to the heavens through the person of Jesus who is the way and door to enter those realms of heaven.

To me, the primary purpose of the coming of Jesus into the world is to open the gates and the door to the heavenly dimension, for me and for all of humanity. The true message of Christianity then is that the door to the heavens has opened to all who, by their freewill, choose to believe the Messiah whom God has sent in the Person of Yeshua (Jesus) Ha-Mashiach (The Christ).

In my journey towards understanding who I am in the Father through the Son, Jesus Christ, I have had many experiences whose examination and analysis, instead of proffering final solutions to intractable spiritual questions, has rather fueled more burning questions.

So rather than offer you a final answer to your questions about the heavens, I hope this book spurs you to ask more questions and to press into the heavens and to search the Scriptures to find more of what the Father has for us as God's Children.

Heaven's Heart for Earth

Seraph Creative is a collective of artists, writers, theologians &
illustrators who desire to see the
body of Christ grow into full maturity, walking
in their inheritance as Sons Of God on the Earth.

Sign up to our newsletter to know about the release of the next book
in the series, as well as other exciting releases.

Visit our website :
www.seraphcreative.org

Made in the USA
Monee, IL
23 December 2020